ARCHITECTURE OF POWER

1ˢᵗ Edition proudly Published by Cymroglyphics, November 2020

Proof reading- Marchell Abrahams

ISBN 970-1-916 2875-3-2

© Cymroglyphics Ltd

10 Lansdale Drive, Tonteg, Pontypridd, Glamorgan, Wales CF38 1PG

ARCHITECTURE OF POWER

by
Robert Shaw

Edited and illustrated by
K. Ross Broadstock

Acknowledgements

I love sharing what I'm interested in, and I want to thank a few people for being such patient listeners.

My fascination with Hawksmoor and the era he worked in has spanned over a decade, for some of my friends it no doubts feels a bit longer than that.

To my family I want to express gratitude for the incredible example you set me. To Sue Denim, my undying love and devotion, it was only after I met you that I was able to write this the right way, with love and humour.

To Robert Richmond, Oliver Ho and Tommy Gillard, thank you for listening, questioning and being the kind of friends that help and support unconditionally.

Lastly, I would like to thank Ross Broadstock, editor, illustrator, friend, mentor and inspiration. Like anything worthwhile, this hasn't always been easy, and Ross's encouragement has moulded my original text in to this book. I will always be grateful.

Robert Shaw

October 2020

Contents

Contents

Contents

Contents

Author's Preface

This book is the result of about a decade of intermittent reading and researching, meandering around the subject, forgetting all about it then coming back as other information emerged.

It is my pleasure to guide you on this unique and perhaps unbelievable journey through London, the city of my birth and nurture. As you may have noticed, as well as making me, London made the modern world: capitalism, science, industrialised war, trade and the global financial empire.

This is personal.

The work of Nicholas Hawksmoor, assistant to Sir Christopher Wren, had popped up a few times in my life, through reading fiction as well as history.

What he was trying to do with the churches he built in London, is an open question, a mystery. Trying to clarify what was man and what was myth took some time. I could not have imagined what my interest in his work would teach me, to be honest I still have trouble believing some of it.

I hope you find the results rewarding, if not always agreeable.

What is clear is that British history, as we on this island are taught it, is full of lies, half-truths and propaganda. This is probably not so different from any other imperial nation, but I don't know enough about their histories to comment.

British history, my heritage as my culture conveyed it to me, is definitively and demonstrably full of falsehoods and omissions, to keep us ignorant of how the great and the good of this country established themselves. This is obviously disappointing, but perhaps not that surprising.

The saying goes behind every great fortune there lies a great crime.

Britain ran the world, and what this entailed has been deliberately hidden from us. What we are taught in our schools and media is at best a half-history, with many glaring omissions. At its worst it's just imperial propaganda.

This book offers a kind of experience that can be unwelcome, can feel intrusive and disruptive.

Learning that Father Christmas isn't real is a fair analogy. Some children cry when they find out, others get a sense of relief at no longer feeling obliged to believe a story that had left them confused. The truth can set you free...

British history, it seems, is full of fictions that some people become emotionally attached to, and there are a fair few jolly dead fat men strewn throughout these pages, and sometimes their pants are showing... sometimes they aren't even wearing any pants...

The facts I've encountered forced me repeatedly to change my mind about what I thought I knew. I recommend it.

Robert Shaw

October 2020

Introduction

Every British child is taught about the 1666 Great Fire of London before we are old enough to question or think about it.

This book demonstrates, beyond reasonable doubt that the official version of these events is a lie, designed to cover up an embarrassing truth.

The Architect Nicholas Hawksmoor (1665-1736) worked in London as assistant to Sir Christopher Wren in the aftermath of the Great Fire. My fascination with Hawksmoor's work is what led me to make some remarkable discoveries about this period.

Using witness statements from the Parliamentary Committee set up to investigate the Great Fire, you'll be shown this era in a context we are never taught. This was part of a sometimes public, sometimes private battle for control of the country, fought between the Crown, in the form of the Stuart Monarchs, and the City of London and the Bankers who ran it.

The City won this battle, became the birth-place for modern Capitalism, and so begat the modern age. Science and technology, industrialised warfare and conquest all helped build the British Empire.

This was all achieved for the enrichment of a small elite who dominated the City.

Today the City remains the single most powerful institution on Earth, all the more so because so few people know it exists, let alone what it is and what it has done. The sixth mass extinction event we are currently experiencing, the destruction of nature and the debt-enslavement of nearly every human on Earth, can be traced back to the Banks of the City of London.

This is the story of how this process was unleashed on the world.

The conflict between the City and the Crown that Hawksmoor was part of is comparable, in some ways, to what was quickly labelled '*Brexit*' in our own times. Two separate elites, with different investments and world-views, were fighting for control of the country.

So, this isn't a good versus evil fairy-story, it's a real history of the rivalry of two powerful groups, fighting messily for control. In the fight between the Aristocrats and Bankers the people were an after-thought, and so we remain.

This 17th century struggle resulted in multiple wars, known collectively today as the 'English Civil War' –

the beheading of King Charles I in 1649,
the restoration of his son Charles II in 1660,
and later the Dutch invasion of this country in 1688,

when King James II was chased off the throne for upsetting the City's business one too many times. The *Glorious Revolution*, as this invasion was called, marked the complete victory of the City over the Crown.

There was a popular rhyme in London in the early 18th Century that went,

"The Lion and the Unicorn,
Fought for the Crown.
The Lion beat the Unicorn
All over town".

This very neatly summarises about 100 hundred years of British politics, the tension between the 'Lions' of the City and the 'Unicorn' Stuart Kings, first James I, then his son, Charles I, and then his two sons Charles II, and last and by all means least, Charles II's younger brother, James II.

As the rhyme states, the Lion beat the Unicorn, which is hardly a surprise. Stuart notions of monarchy were based on superstition and convention. The City is and was only ever a pragmatic body.

It's worth keeping in mind that Charles II and James II, the last two Stuart Kings, returned to rule a country that had rebelled against and executed their father. They had been routinely defeated and humiliated on the battlefield by the people they had later returned to reign over.

For the ultra status-conscious Stuarts, this was supremely awkward.

These Stuart brothers believed they had a *Divine Right* to rule over their subjects: as man obeys God – without question – so a subject should obey their King. From their point of view the people who had humiliated them and beheaded their father, had not just committed regicide, they had committed deicide – had killed God.

This book puts forward the hypothesis that this was not something the Stuart Brothers found it easy to forgive, and they plotted their revenge on a scale unimaginable to most people.

The traumatised tend to share their trauma with others; these young men were obviously and understandably scarred. It seems they may have created death and destruction on a deliberately Biblical scale: they focussed their plans on the place they blamed for their father's execution: the City of London.

Caveat Emptor

There are thousands of books, videos and online lectures that make sensationalist, revisionist claims. They range from the sane to the deranged: from saying the British Empire destroyed the Indian economy, an undeniable fact; to the idea that the Queen is a lizard.

So how can you have any assurance what you are reading is reliable?

What constitutes evidence when talking about 'hidden' history, given we cannot go back in time and check for ourselves?

First-hand accounts of events are an excellent source, but may be subject to the vagaries of memory and individual bias.

Written records from the time are useful, but will also reflect the attitudes of whoever wrote them. Obviously if a particular historian was being paid to write, knowing who employed them will tell us a lot about possible biases.

The suggestions and opinions offered herein are based on the facts as I found them. I never, ever expected to find out what I did about our history. You won't believe it, I can't blame you, at first neither could I.

Like the child who was glad to understand Santa-Claus was all a story, even if it meant fewer presents, so the more mature me was relieved, but not happy as such, to be released from the fetters of our collective memory – our history – much of which is unreliable, and doesn't make sense when you think about it...

This book will try to highlight some of the glaring omissions in how British history is taught. These omissions are so egregious that something suspicious must lie behind them. Huge parts of our history are never even mentioned. When you see what the official story leaves out, it becomes obvious a deliberate lie has been promulgated.

It's always important to look at our own biases. Some people identify with power structures and seek to defend them, others are iconoclasts and look for any excuse to criticise the corruption of others, never considering what this might say about themselves.

There are 'social/oxytocin junkies' who adopt the official position and rise through hierarchies of orthodox opinion. They rarely ever say anything new or interesting, it is their job to echo established verities.

Then there are the 'stimulation/adrenaline junkies' who look for reasons to be scared and excited, seek out conspiracies and find them everywhere. These people allow themselves flights of fantasy, starting with a stimulating conclusion and schizophrenically cherry picking anything that can keep them in their heightened state.

One is the pursuit of social status, the other the abandonment of reality for stimulation.

This is to say I have tried, the best I can, to avoid either of these two types of error, and taken a middle course. Some say rules are there to be obeyed, for others, rules are there to be broken; I've tried to take the attitude that the rules are just there. Information should be the only basis for reaching historical conclusions, not a desire to reinforce, or destroy, convention for its own sake.

The best analogy I can think of is that of the Actuary, that grey eminence at the insurance company who works out just how likely something is.

Imagine trying to tell an insurance company that the greatest writer in the world couldn't sign his own name.

That's what our history says. I am fore-shadowing what is to come.

Sometimes a single piece of evidence is enough to shake the foundations of our understanding, to force us to reconsider what we thought we knew. Something sticks out as anomalous or counter-intuitive and begs questions that our existing narrative cannot accommodate.

Like an actuary assessing a claim we should be pragmatic, believe nothing and *accommodate all the evidence.*

So, by way of introduction to the rest of this book I will offer two examples from the history of the era. One being the question of who wrote the plays attributed to William Shakespeare, the other being the events surrounding the 'Gunpowder Plot' that made Guy Fawkes so famous.

These did not happen as we are conventionally taught, and I hope describing them will be interesting for their own sake, indicative of the approach of the rest of the book, as well as offering famous examples of British history not being what we are told it is.

After sharing these examples of this *actuarial* approach, I will outline what got me interested in this era in the first place, the *poetry* of Nicholas Hawksmoor's London churches.

Trying to understand those buildings gradually opened my eyes to what was happening at that time.

Chapter 1
Shakespeare couldn't write?!

Shakespeare's place at the heart of British culture needs no explanation, but, remarkably, it is not based in fact, and this is very easy to establish.

One incontrovertible fact was enough to convince me to re-examine everything I thought I knew about him. I will put this to you, a glove across your face, as it was across mine.

A challenge.

If this doesn't do something good for you, then I suggest you shouldn't read this book, as the historical conclusions I reach are based on this type of actuarial, scientific, evidence-led approach. Conventional narratives have no value in the face of contradictory and irrefutable evidence.

Evidence must absolutely trump opinion. That the Royal Society, for example, use the Latin slogan "Nullius in Verba", *take no one's word for it.* No amount of expert opinion or tradition is equal to one established fact.

A single observation in science can change our whole understanding of the world we live in. When Galileo looked through his telescope and saw moons orbiting Jupiter, it proved that the Earth was not the centre of the Universe.

Just look at these:

These are found in witnessed legal documents: they are undoubtedly the signature of William Shakespeare, the son of a glover maker from Stratford upon Avon, and the world's greatest writer.[1]

This is also *everything* we have that William Shakespeare wrote.

Apart from these signatures, that hardly resemble each other and demonstrate very poor control of a pen, *nothing else exists in his handwriting.*

This from the greatest writer to have ever lived?

It was much easier for me to dismiss this fact when I first came across it. This is called *cognitive dissonance* but I prefer the phrase *lazy-brain.*

It takes a lot of effort to assimilate this sort of idea, it takes work, so generally we don't bother, and find an easy way out. I immediately began to try to contextualise and dismiss it.

So what?, I thought, *he lived long ago, maybe all his other writings have just been lost though time.*

But, unfortunately for my lazy brain, that is not the case with any other notable poet from the era.

They were writers, their product was always, at least initially, handwritten. There are reams of paper, precious folios, by Ben Johnson, Christopher Marlowe and Edmund Spencer, for example.

Even more obscure figures like Thomas Nashe and Samuel Daniel, contemporaries of Shakespeare's, left copious amounts of script in their own hand-writing. There's nothing like that from Shakespeare. This seemed extremely strange, almost unbelievable, and took me a while to process. How could it be the greatest writer ever either didn't or couldn't write using his own hands?!

The history of Shakespeare states he would present the plays to his actors in 'fair copy', meaning they were neatly written, without crossings-out or amendments of any kind. This has become part of the legend of his genius, he wrote some of the greatest works of literature without making a single mistake, never needing to correct himself, without ever making a last-minute amendment or improvement.

This was unprecedented and is unbelievable.

13

Shakespeare running from Autograph hunters

Sir Mark Rylance, the actor and Artistic Director of the Globe Theatre from 1995-2005, recommends reading "Shakespeare's Unorthodox Biography", by Diana Price, which details dozens of anomalies in the official Shakespeare history. It is a forensic and illuminating read.

Some think the plays were actually by Edward de Vere, 17th Earl of Oxford. There are precedents for this, in ancient Rome aristocrats who wished to publish their plays, but who wanted to remain anonymous, would hire someone to pretend to be the writer. This person was called a Batillus.

Many plays were performed for Queen Elizabeth I at court, and de Vere wrote some of them. There were, no doubt, several people who hoped to win the Queen's favour by staging such entertainments. These plays were, others suggest, later collated by the statesman

Francis Bacon and used to publish the first folio of Shakespeare's work in 1623, seven years after Shakespeare had died.

The details of the authorship question are still debated among academics. The actor Sir Derek Jacobi describes it as the *"greatest literary whodunit of all time"*. It's a fascinating episode.

What matters here is this: if you reject the notion of Shakespeare being unable to sign his own name, I ask you to think about what you are rejecting, and the basis on which you are doing so. Tradition is trumping evidence: you are obeying your memory, not processing the information in front of you.

The signatures above are the only writing we have we know is definitely in Shakespeare's hand, this is unequivocal fact. There were witnesses. This evidence shows he had trouble signing his own name and no amount of conjecture or expert opinion can explain this away.

Any understanding of history must start from the evidence we have, and the fact is he, William Shakespeare, could not control a pen with anything like the fluency of today's average five year-old.

This fact cannot be debunked or dismissed in a credible account of his life and work, but, incredibly, it is always ignored. The orthodox history of Shakespeare is, therefore, more of a hagiography than a history. We have the fairy-tale story of a poor-boy making it good in the big smoke.

Trying to fit new information into existing memories doesn't always work and is no way to get to the truth, is not a theory of knowledge that bears any scrutiny. Opinions and traditions are like hearsay, and as such, should be inadmissible as evidence.

Look at the signatures of the "world's greatest writer", this is all we have of his writing. If this doesn't make you question what you were told at school and other orthodox channels, I cannot see how you'd profit from reading this book.

Those who are temperamentally inclined to reject the evidence that Shakespeare couldn't use a pen are left in an absurd position.

They have to say all the other evidence of Shakespeare's writing has been destroyed, unlike any other poet of the age, and despite the fact anyone who had the least scrap of his writing would have known it had value. Were all of Shakespeare's handwritten works destroyed by accident? Ridiculous.

More far-fetched still is the idea that those signatures, all on witnessed legal documents, were made when Shakespeare was ill in some undetermined way that made his hands shake?

Shakespeare got the shakes whenever he had to sign his name?

That is just not credible for the greatest writer to have ever lived. It is much more likely he was an actor paid to impersonate an author, someone who could read but not write. He owned no books when he died.

Nor did any contemporary writer celebrate his life.

When he died, there was no fanfare, no mourning the loss of this most amazing of talents. It wasn't until his plays were printed seven years later that Ben Johnson and others celebrated his genius.

This was also unprecedented. Poets of the age commemorated the achievements of their peers upon their passing. It seems at the time of his death he was friendless and forgotten.

But this is not the popular image, which has been crafted to make Shakespeare likable, the diamond in the rough that shone through.

It's much more likely the principle writer of the 'Shakespeare' plays, who had detailed knowledge of law, Italy, Court politics and falconry, was an aristocrat. Not the son of a glove-maker made good, whose parents and children were all illiterate.

No matter the social stigma that may accompany it, the old Bardic mantra of *"Y Gwir Yn Erbyn Y Byd", the truth against the world*, must be the approach of anyone trying to establish anything. This takes a bit of time and effort, to do what the Buddhists do and *un*learn, chip away at the edifice of ideas built in your mind whilst you were younger.

So much for Shakespeare. Suffice to say, if you don't care about the truth enough to ruffle some mental feathers, you should flutter off now. If you want to know more, Diana Price's book is amazingly thorough, and her lectures are on Youtube.

If you're up for being entertained, however, you could do worse than watch *Anonymous*, by Roland Emmerich, the director of *Independence Day*. It offers an explosive and melodramatic version of the "Shakespeare" story. Interestingly in *Anonymous* the Cecil family play a significant role, as they are about to again.

Unicorn King

The first Stuart King, James I, was the son of Mary Stuart, who was executed by Elizabeth I, and Henry Stuart, also known as Lord Darnley, who was likely killed by being smothered with a pillow, after an abortive assassination attempt had failed to blow him up.

James I, child of these ill-fated parents, was quite understandably a bit jumpy and spent most of his life fearing he too would be killed. He was small, weak and plagued by nightmares. He was so terrified of witches that he wrote a book, *The Daemonology*,[2] about defeating them. He was clearly more superstitious than rational. This made him easy to manipulate.

The Stuarts' possession of the Crown from 1603 until 1714 saw some momentous events; so many I want to list them again, this time using bullet points:
- The Civil Wars 1642-1651;
- The execution of Charles I in 1649;
- The Republic under Cromwell from 1649-1660;
- The Restoration of Charles II in 1660;
- James II, brother of Charles II, being chased off the throne during The Glorious Revolution, in 1688;
- The abrupt ending of the Stuart line by handing the crown to the person who was the 57th in line for it, George I, of the House of Hanover, in 1715.[3]

So it's worth taking a moment to look at the first Stuart King in a little detail. James I of England was also James VI of Scotland, and for the first time the two nations had one ruler.

This event was seen in Biblical terms by a population whose main source of information was still the *Good Book*. James, famously, had the Bible rewritten. The King James Version, commissioned by him, emphasized the place of Bishops, a subject to which we'll return.

James apparently loved debating the finer points of religious doctrine and considered himself an expert. He was celebrated by sycophants as a new Solomon, bringing peace and prosperity to the 'chosen' people of Britain. As narcissistic and deranged as this might sound, James was not above this kind of grand notion about himself. No science tempered his imagination; he was deeply superstitious. Perhaps never more so than about himself.

Apart from *The Daemonology*, James wrote a book about kingship, called the *Basilicon Doron*, which is Greek for 'Royal Gift'.[4]

This was nominally written for his eldest son Henry, who later died, but it was also made available to the public and was James' manifesto for the way he thought kingship, and therefore religion and government, should be. It included his belief that he could heal the sick of 'scrofula' by touching them.

The most important aspect of his outlook was his belief in the Divine Right of Kings, that God had ordained his fate, that it was God's will that he was king, he was chosen. In the *Basilicon Doron* James says that even God saw kings as like little gods. They were cut from a different cloth from the rest of humanity.

This Divine Right to rule was certainly a convenient fiction for a weak and insecure personality like James. What's important for this story is that he brought that attitude to England when he became king.

All the Stuart Monarchs thought they were above the law, just as God is above his creation, so the king is above the state. What's interesting is that no Divine Right tradition ever really existed in Scotland, the Declaration of Arbroath of 1320 had ruled this out.

As James VI he was king of Scots, but only on a first amongst equals basis.

So, somewhere, somehow James adopted a philosophy that was alien both to Scotland and England, an approach that was at variance with the traditional freedoms and liberties that had been celebrated, if not enjoyed, from time immemorial. Where and how James developed this idea of himself as divine is hard to say definitively, but there are certainly some obvious places to start.

Famously James's *favourite*, which in his case meant lover, was an apparently very dashing young man called Robert Carr. James was often open to ideas that Carr suggested. Carr was known to be under the influence of one Sir Thomas Overbury, and Overbury was known to be in the service of Robert Cecil. Cecil had done more than anyone else to make James King of England[5].

Robert Cecil, son of William Cecil, was at the cold heart of the Royal Court. Both had served Queen Elizabeth as her most trusted advisors. As the Queen aged, the Cecils slowly arranged the Stuart succession. In London, these Scottish Kings would need to rely on the Cecils, as they were alien to the English Court and nobility, with no allies and no one else to turn to. Part of the Cecils' role in protecting the King was to regulate his vices, to keep them private, to have control.

So Robert Cecil controlled Robert Carr, who pretty much controlled the King. When Robert Cecil died in 1612, James' wife, Anne of Denmark, worked to have Robert Parr replaced by one George Villiers, who James later made Duke of Buckingham. Villiers was, at least at first, more under Anne's control, and as such was preferable to her than Parr[6].

Point being James was pretty easy to manipulate, and people at court understandably conspired to do this. So, James' ideas about Divine Right style government, it seems, might have been nurtured by Cecil's agent Carr. This outlook suited Cecil's view of the state as all-powerful: that its might gave it the right.

On March 25th, 1603, James was proclaimed King of England.

He had a high opinion of himself in matters scriptural, and was inclined toward clemency for his Catholic subjects. It was clear James hoped to ease the plight of his Catholic subjects and rule all his people. He married his daughters to both Catholic and Protestant Princes in Europe.

He was a bridge builder, a conciliator and consistently ineffective at foreign policy, much of which was based on religious affiliation. He perhaps hoped to be a unifying influence.

Then in 1605, so the story goes, a bunch of Catholic fanatics tried to blow up the Houses of Parliament with James in it.

Robert Cecil, 1st Earl of Salisbury (1563 – 1612)

Chapter 2
Who staged the Gunpowder plot?

Before even coming to London, James had hinted that he might relax some of the restrictions placed on Catholics by Elizabeth I. This was deeply troubling to Robert Cecil, whose family fortune had been made suppressing the '*Popish fanatics*' by confiscating their lands and property.

England's identity as a Protestant mercantilist state, as shepherded by the Cecils under Elizabeth, was in potential jeopardy. Robert Cecil made sure this did not happen, and every year since we've burnt effigies and set off fire-works to celebrate his success.

As with the Shakespeare authorship question I am not going to lay out a detailed analysis, but highlight unequivocal facts that fatally undermine the official version of events. Again, this isn't hard to do, even some children's history books point these things out.

Firstly, after Guy Fawkes was caught, on November 5th, it took two days before he would even give his name. That he was tortured cannot seriously be doubted, but he held out on even giving his name until the 7th.

It took over a week to extract all the names of his accomplices, chief among those he incriminated were Robert Catesby and Thomas Percy.

After Fawkes' arrest, his co-conspirators gathered at Holbeche House, 120 miles away from London, near Dudley in the West Midlands. Somehow, on the 8th November, before Fawkes had even given the authorities their names, soldiers had surrounded, then arrested or killed all the other plotters.

The first thing to point out is, we are never really told this part of the story, the aftermath of Fawkes' arrest was an *unbelievable* cock-up, with the plotters turning from would-be terrorists into incompetent clowns.

Rather than split up they decided to try and spark a Catholic rebellion. They raided Warwick castle for weapons and made about as much noise as possible. This alerted the authorities! Instead of trying to disappear they provoked the authorities into chasing them.

The High Sheriff of Worcestershire, Sir Richard Walsh, set out to find them, with 700 men, on the 6th November.

The official version of events is that a couple of days later, on the 8th, when the Sheriff and his men were nearby the plotters accidentally blew themselves up, destroying much of Holbeche House.

They had been trying to dry gunpowder using a fire, and it had gone wrong, at just the wrong time. The plotters were then arrested or killed.

Lots of people at the time said this was suspicious, not least the Earl of Northumberland who, to his surprise, was arrested for his part in the plot. He was kept in the Tower of London for fifteen years, nearly executed, and, understandably, was very upset, given he was innocent.

Catholics in England were also utterly dismayed by the Plot, and they would be persecuted for generations as a result of it. They all had their doubts about the plotters' motivations.

What follows is my summary of the work of Francis Edwards, a Jesuit who researched the era, specifically the work of Robert Cecil. He wrote books about the Gunpowder Plot, as well as the Bye and Main Plots, and the Essex Rebellion, which we'll look at in a moment. All of these occurred between 1601 and 1603.

Robert Cecil was working to ensure James Stuart would succeed Elizabeth. Many died as a direct result of Cecil's ruthless cunning. Francis Edwards' research is based on documents from the time, and these show how different the reality was from the official version of events.

The two principle plotters were Thomas Percy and Robert Catesby; the plot was their idea. They both had form, and had been part of the Essex Rebellion, when the Earl of Essex, the dashing Robert Devereux, had tried to take the throne from Queen Elizabeth in 1601.

The Earl, it seems, believed himself to be the illegitimate son of the 'Virgin Queen', and a better successor than James I. Cecil squashed this revolt, he wanted a King that would rely on him and the popular Essex was executed.

This Essex Rebellion also shines an interesting light on the relationship 'Shakespeare' had with Robert Cecil. The day before the rebellion, February 8th 1601, a play was performed at the Globe. It depicted a hunch-back Machiavellian schemer, who murdered and lied himself to the throne. The name of this play, *Richard III*, did not confuse its audience.

Robert Cecil, a hunch-back Machiavellian schemer, was being portrayed. It seems the performance included new, more topical and satirical material than in previous versions of the play. The real Richard III was not a cripple, but Cecil was, the character was used to attack Cecil by proxy: it was a character assassination. The crowd were deliberately whipped up into a violent frenzy and hundreds poured out of the theatre to join Essex's ranks.

The play was a devastating satire upon Robert Cecil, and the portrayal of corruption at the highest levels of government was used to foment rebellion. Perhaps this is why 'Shakespeare' was completely ignored by his peers when he died six years later?

This it also highlights how much Cecil must have hated *Macbeth* in 1603, which was written for his chosen successor to Elizabeth's throne, James I. Despite palpable links to a treasonous rebellion *Shakespeare* dedicated the play to his new king. James was so pleased with it he promoted the whole acting company.

Cecil, it would appear, decided to create a real-life drama of his own.

After the Essex Rebellion was put down Percy and Catesby were arrested, the punishment for treason was death, but they survived. So why weren't they executed? Because, Francis Edwards suggests, Robert Cecil made them an offer they couldn't refuse, *"Come and work for me and we'll postpone your executions for as long as you are of service"*.

This is one explanation for the clemency that was shown to Percy and Catesby, I'm open to other suggestions, but the state did not often commute a death sentence for treason, especially for people of low rank. Cecil had recruited other agents this way. If nothing else it was a remarkable act of clemency from a man known for cold-blooded efficiency.

So, *at very least*, the two principles in the Gunpowder Plot should have been sentenced to death, but had *somehow* lived.

Almost immediately after their release Catesby and Percy went around finding fellow Catholics who might be interested in blowing up parliament. They focussed their attentions on families close to the Earl of Northumberland, whose surname was also Percy. The Earl was an implacable foe of Robert Cecil, and after the plot was exposed, Cecil used the fact that families close to the Earl had been involved to have him imprisoned.

James was shaken, ready to condemn on the basis of guilt by association, and Cecil successfully killed several birds with the one stone. Cecil repeatedly, but unsuccessfully, tried to persuade James to execute the Earl.

As Catesby and Percy went around as 'tame ducks to attract wild geese', the group of conspirators grew, with Guy Fawkes one of the last to join. Catesby and Percy also went out of their way to confess what they were doing to as many Jesuit priests as they could. These confessions caused widespread dismay amongst these Jesuits, who were sworn to keep confessions secret: they could not tell the authorities as this would break the sacred trust they held.

The Jesuits confessed to each other about it, however; there are letters to and from Jesuits in England and the Continent decrying the plotters and what their actions would mean for Catholics across the country. These are a matter of record.[7]

The Jesuits tried everything they could to stop Catesby and Percy's plot, knowing full well it was spell disaster for English Catholicism. This is remarkable given in many British 'histories' the Jesuits are blamed, even demonised, for inspiring the plot. *The very opposite is the truth.*

After the plot was discovered all the priests that had heard Catesby's and Percy's confessions were arrested and questioned. Someone in authority had a list of names, presumably supplied by Catesby and Percy themselves. The priests were asked if they had known about the plot, they all answered they had. They were asked why they hadn't alerted the authorities, and they all answered that would violate confession and their oaths.

These Jesuits were executed. Some were hung, drawn and quartered just for good measure.

That all happened later. On November 8th 1605, before Fawkes had given up their names, the conspirators at Holbeche House held a meeting. Thomas Percy had prepared the room that morning, in the centre was a barrel with a metal lid, or platter, with holes in. Around this barrel Percy had arranged stools and a bench.

As his co-conspirators woke and gathered in the meeting room Percy suggested he fetch a brazier to see off the morning chill. He returned with the fire-bucket and a poker. Catesby and others warmed themselves as Percy then said he would bring them all hot cordials to drink.[8]

It seems Catesby then started to poke the fire and some of the burning embers fell into the barrel.

What Percy had forgotten to tell his friends was that he had put two linen bags, holding about thirty pounds of gunpowder into the barrel, and then packed lots of papers around them.

One bag exploded, blowing the roof off, and everyone in the room was burned. If the second bag had gone off it is doubtful any of them would have survived, except Percy, of course, who was getting them their cordials.

The Attorney General, Sir Edward Coke, who described this incredible event, was able to detail the fate of the second bag of gunpowder with amazing accuracy.

"The powder taking fire and blowing up, scorched those who were nearest... blew up the roof of the house; and the linen bag which was set under the platter being therewith suddenly carried out through the breach, fell down in the courtyard whole and unfired; which if it had took fire in the room, would have slain them all there, so that they never should have come to... trial."[9]

The only explosion connected with the Gunpowder Plot of 1605 nearly killed all the plotters, and alerted the local Sheriff to their whereabouts.

Soon the plotters were surrounded. Some surrendered, but apparently not Catesby and Percy. The official version of events is that they fought on to the death. Perhaps this is true, but given the fact they were both killed by the same bullet, it sounds more like an execution.

Cecil granted the lucky marksman who dispatched them a pension of forty Shillings a year for life.

The plot was officially discovered by Cecil after a Lord Monteagle received a letter warning him not to attend the opening of Parliament. Monteagle showed this to Cecil on October 26th, but Cecil didn't order a search until Fawkes was in place, over a week later.

Unsurprisingly, gunpowder was not readily available in large quantities. All of London's powder was supposed to be kept in the Tower of London. Where Fawkes got his thirty-six barrels is not clear as the Tower's records for that year went missing.[10]

The letters Edwards cites between Jesuits make it clear: the people who were officially blamed for the plot were not part of it, and were desperate to try and stop it.

There is no letter from Cecil saying how he created and executed the plot, but who would expect such evidence to exist?

With Shakespeare, who should have written thousands, even millions of words in his life, and only left us those signatures, there is a ridiculous lack of evidence for him as a writer.

With Guy Fawkes there is clear evidence that the official narrative at the time was a lie, the *Jesuits did not create the plot*; Catesby and Percy did, and their actions were reckless, incompetent and hard to comprehend without more context than we're normally given.

The Plot was orchestrated by Cecil to convince James that Catholicism could not be tolerated. As a consequence of his deft handling of the situation, Cecil was also able to discredit the Earl of Northumberland, one of his most vigorous opponents at Court. With Catesby and Percy dead, there was no way to connect him to the events.

This is how Catesby and Percy got away with it. They were known to the authorities – *who had had their death sentences commuted* – had plotted away with little discretion, incriminating everyone they could, and would get away with it until they were no longer of service. This wider context, and the unbelievable coincidence of soldiers and plotters and explosions at Holbeche House, makes the official story unsustainable.

If you can't believe that Robert Cecil could be that cold-hearted and calculated, that manipulative and ruthless, then I suggest you look up what he did to his friend Sir Walter Rayleigh, or his brother-in-law Henry Brook. The opinion of the Bishop of Gloucester, Dr Godfrey Goodman, was that Cecil would "first contrive and then discover a treason".

Looking in

These sorts of combinations of anomalies and incongruities deserve scrutiny. This scrutinising of the past helps us see through the stuff we're told by people trying to manipulate us today. Understanding politics and understanding humanity is the same thing, and at a bit of a distance you see things that you could miss close up.

Looking critically at Britain's history exposes us to some dark corners and unpleasant truths. Like finding out about the skeletons in the closet of a friend or relative, these revelations are often highly illuminating and leave us better equipped to deal with reality.

There's no Actuary in the world that would accept these Shakespeare and Guy Fawkes stories as history. They are, as we are taught them, as much fable as fact.

The way these sorts of things are calculated is by compounding probabilities, so in Shakespeare's case, the claim is he was the world's greatest writer. We have to factor in that he couldn't sign his name, didn't own a book, left no manuscripts, was not celebrated at his death, and so on, and give these factors a weighting.

These weightings represent how likely something is, then you multiply these together to get an overall probability. Here let's say each of these factors are one thousand to one against: factoring only these four points, and giving them a simple rating that *underplays* how unlikely they are, the results are still one trillion to one.

It is a very rough figure made on the back of an envelope, but it illustrates the process. And neither Shakespeare's nor Guy Fawkes' stories can be said to pass this kind of test.

This type of thinking was the furthest thing from my mind when I first looked at Hawksmoor's churches. There was something mysterious, eldritch and obscure about them. They featured in fiction as occult centres, powerful symbols of unknown significance. In architectural books they were described as idiosyncratic, eccentric, anomalous and bizarre.

Whatever Hawksmoor was up to was it was categorically *poetic*, not something that could be analysed in terms of probability. You can't understand a picture by focussing in one individual pixel, can't understand a song by hearing one note, you have to stand back and experience holistically, the big picture, the context.

When looking holistically one looks for connotations, external links and connections. This contrasts with the denotations, coherence and logic one applies when thinking actuarially.

These two processes, according to neuroscience, carried out by the two hemispheres of the brain: the left tends to analyse, the right contextualise. 'The Master and his Emissary' by Iain MacGilchirst sets this out, an epistemology based on neuroscience.

When it comes to what Hawksmoor was trying to do this books offers a theory that cannot really be disproved, it is an interpretation of his intentions that are now unknowable – he never recorded why he did what he did. Set in the context I will offer, I hope my suggestion will at least seem less ridiculous.

This suggestion, however, does accommodate all the facts the actuarial part of the book uncovers, and uses them as a starting point for conjecture. There is a lot of conjecture; the theory requires a certain amount of setting to make sense. Trying to make sense of these churches and their context in history is what this has always been about for me.

Interior of St Alphege's

Chapter 3
The Mind's Eye
The plan behind Hawksmoor's buildings

I did not wake up one day and decide that some famous *history* as we are taught it is clearly wrong, false, disinformation. I think it is only fair to be sceptical of the powerful, what they say and what they do. But the journey down this rabbit hole began for me with an urban legend about the work of an obscure architect, Nicholas Hawksmoor (1665-1736), who had been Sir Christopher Wren's assistant.

What he did in London was well established, what was less clear was why he had bothered.

About fifteen years ago I was teaching at Christchurch Primary School on Brick Lane, a Church of England School full of Muslim children. I asked Margaret Hewson, who had worked in the school for thirty-five years, why the school, that was 100% Muslim, was connected to the Church of England, why these poor kids were having to sing hymns in assembly and hear parables about Jesus when they were all Muslim.

Marge told me about a tunnel that ran between the school and a church 100 yards away on Commercial Street, Hawksmoor's Christchurch. The school and the Church were linked historically and architecturally.

It dawned on me that this school was connected to one of the best novels I'd ever read.

Peter Ackroyd's *Hawksmoor*, features a crypto-satanic architect who builds a series of churches to cast some kind of spell on London.

If you don't know his work, Ackroyd's *London the Biography* is the best book about this City, his *Histories of England* series offers frank insight into the development of this country, and his *Albion, The Origins of the English Imagination*, traces the evolution of the English written tradition.

Hawksmoor's Towers, Westminster Abbey
Photograph by the Author

In his novel *Hawksmoor*, Ackroyd had an architect build a labyrinth "to last a thousand years" beneath Christchurch, and suddenly I knew there was a tunnel right where Ackroyd had said it was.

As I was stood on the corner of Brick Lane and Fournier Street, with Marge, I felt an overwhelming urge to go full Indiana Jones and investigate.

I asked Andy, the Rector of Christchurch, if I could go down the tunnel, and mentioned Ackroyd's book. This clearly hit a nerve with him; he said the Church had no time for idle conspiracy theories in a way that felt well rehearsed.

Hawksmoor's Churches also feature in *From Hell*, Alan Moore's genius rendition of the Jack the Ripper murders. The Parish Council had clearly had enough of Hawksmoor enthusiasts bothering them with their strange theories.

The idea of the tunnel fascinated me, but I couldn't see any way to get down there, except by breaking in, something I didn't feel I could to do.

A few months later a friend suggested it might make a good documentary, and if I did some more research, maybe he could help me get it made. fifteen years later, and that idle chatter over beer has somehow yet to materialise, but I did do some research.

I read some books:

Kerry Downes' 'Hawksmoor', and Vaughan Hart's 'Nicholas Hawksmoor', serious and somewhat sesquipedalian architectural histories of the real man's work.

Born in 1661, he had had an amazing career, plucked out of obscurity at seventeen, he became Sir Christopher Wren's assistant during the rebuilding of St Paul's Cathedral after the Great Fire of 1666. Aged forty-six, his supporters in Parliament passed a bill that enabled him to build his London churches. He was a generation younger than and a social class beneath Wren, and Hawksmoor has long remained in his master's shadow.

There had never been a better time to be an English architect. As well as building in London, Hawksmoor worked on Blenheim Palace and

Castle Howard, two of the most famous Great Houses in England. His most famous work being his last, the Towers of Westminster Abbey.

When it came to Hawksmoor's London Churches I was looking for references to their locations, as this had been a theme in both Ackroyd's novel and *From Hell*. Where the churches were located was important in the fictional accounts, and, it turns out, it mattered to the real Hawksmoor too. Ackroyd and others call this *Psychogeography*.

For example, Hawksmoor had spent months trying to acquire a piece of land in Wapping, about a hundred yards to the west of where the church he built now stands. He tried persuasion, offered a very good price, but was refused. His supporters in the aristocracy tried to flex their muscle and force a sale, but this too failed.

Why did this matter?

Intriguingly, the factual books I read about Hawksmoor describe his churches as best understood "*of a piece*", and that they were "*sermons in stone*". Together the churches tell a story. Kerry Downes, Vaughan Hart, Alan Moore and Peter Ackroyd had implied things, but none of them clearly articulated what it was, in their opinion, Hawksmoor was really trying to do.

I knew Hawksmoor had built six Churches and helped design the spires for two more. I opened up Google Earth and plotted them.

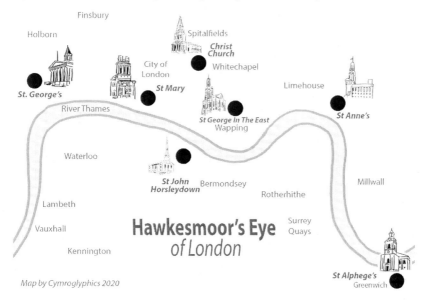

Map by Cymroglyphics 2020

Of the seven churches shown on the map Hawksmoor designed and six by himself, the seventh, St John's Horsleydown, he built with his apprentice John James. St John's was badly damaged by repeated bombings and pulled down after World War Two. All the other churches remain more or less intact. This distribution of churches is what the poet Iain Sinclair called the 'shape of fear' in his epic poem Sinclair's insight that inspired Alan Moore to feature Hawksmoor's work in 'From Hell'. Ackroyd took Sinclair's idea and ran away with it in his novel Hawksmoor. What was so inspiring about this strange game of join the dots?

The four churches in the middle make a kind of tilted square. If the Church in Wapping had been built about 100 yards to the west, as Hawksmoor had wanted, the distance between the four churches, the four sides of the square, would have been equal to within a few yards.

Why bother?

Greenwich observatory with the City of London looming over it
(Watercolour-KRB 2000)

My answer to this question, my theory, this story, is that Hawksmoor built his churches to achieve something greater than the sum of its parts. Getting my head round this was literally psychedelic for me; it expanded my mind, my understanding of London, Architecture, Religion, History and Freemasonry.

Some claim the distribution of Hawksmoor churches is just random, that any pattern is purely in the eye of the beholder. But there is a simple demonstration that this cannot have been the case, and that, for whatever reason, the placement of his churches was deeply important to him.

Sir Christopher Wren had been instructed to design The Royal Naval Hospital at Greenwich. The day-to-day running of the works was Hawksmoor's duty. Wren, an astronomer by training who'd taken up architecture later in life, needed someone practical, someone to engineer his ideas.

Hawksmoor's problems here in Greenwich had started over fifty years before, when Queen Anne of Denmark had shot the beloved dog of her husband, King James I. The story goes the King built the Queen's House to apologise, having sworn in front of his wife after she had somehow shot his poor prized pooch. The story is almost certainly apocryphal. She shot his dog dead, he swore, so he built her a house?

This was 1612, the year Robert Cecil died and Robert Carr – James' favourite – was being edged out by George Villiers. James and Anne's was not a happy marriage. A dog may, or may not, have been shot, but Anne got the house built.

It's a strange home. It seems like one building from the outside, but the road that runs through and under the centre of the house splits it into two separate apartments, with little connection between them. Symbolic of the marriage, perhaps.

Wren had been charged with erecting a Naval Hospital befitting the grandeur of the Royal Navy. The problem of how to build around The Queen's House became Hawksmoor's.

What matters to this story is the lay-out of the whole. It is built along an axis of symmetry set by the orientation of the Queen's House. Every major part of this complex of buildings conforms to this symmetrical arrangement.

This arrangement extends up the hill to Blackheath Avenue to the south, and is not controversial.

What you're about to see next is, officially, just a coincidence.

My theory is based on the idea this sort of placement was central to what Hawksmoor was trying to do, and not coincidental. For some reason this has become controversial, and the water has been muddied by enthusiasts for Alan Moore's and Peter Ackroyd's fictional renderings of him.

It demonstrates that co-ordinating the placement of the churches was crucial to him.

Or why bother doing this?

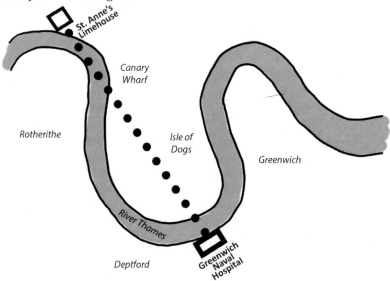

If you follow the line of symmetry to the North then, over a mile away in Limehouse the line crosses Hawksmoor's church St Anne's.

View from Greenwich hill showing direct line to St. Anne's
Photograph by the author

This line is good to within a foot or so of the spire. Before the building of Canary Wharf this alignment could be seen from Greenwich Hill, it seems obvious that this was deliberate.

Hawksmoor bought the land St Anne's was built on - he chose the spot. 'Coincidence' seems like a poor excuse for a reason, or dissembling.

Greenwich Observatory

The view from Greenwich Hill is the best view of London, and where I suggest you go if you want to contemplate this City.

The view when Hawksmoor arrived in the late 1680s, was stark. London was struggling to remake itself. In 1666, thirteen-thousand houses and eighty-seven churches had burnt down. This was all being remade, in stone or brick, as London became the biggest building site in the world.

Masons from all over the globe converged here; you find the same mason's mark on the Taj Mahal as you do St Paul's Cathedral, quite a cool C.V.! London became the biggest building site in the world.

The reconstruction was swift and not always scrupulous, developers using their work-forces to press claims on dubiously owned land.

For Wren, and later Hawksmoor, the Great Fire offered an opportunity of a life-time, to rebuild London, as the Capital of Empire, from scratch, with wide roads and magnificent vistas, celebrating the Glory of God, King and Nation. But commercial reality overtook them, and their greater plans were frustrated.

Later Hawksmoor wrote, in the wake of the fire, London should have become…

"A convenient regular, well built city, excellent, skilful, honest artificers made by the greatness and quantity of the work in rebuilding such a capital. But instead of these we have, no city, no streets, no houses, but a chaos of dirty rotten sheds, always tumbling or taking fire, with windy crooked passages (scarce practicable) lakes of mud and rills of stinking mire running through them." (11)

Statements like this from Hawksmoor seemed odd to me, they stuck with me because he did not refer to the fire as a tragic catastrophe, as you might expect, but as a lost opportunity, and specifically as an opportunity to recruit and train masons.

The scale of rebuilding offered a chance to train a generation of '*honest artificers*' – stonemasons – who would be employed in remaking the City. He hoped London would be made '*A convenient regular*' city, built to a new over-arching street plan. But this did

40

not happen, and Hawksmoor was not alone in thinking this God-given opportunity had been missed.

As I learnt about Hawksmoor and his circle of associates, especially Wren and his friend Robert Hooke, I began to see there was a bigger story, a context which gave new meaning to events.

I have described my theory about Hawksmoor's churches at the end of the book. As it turns out, as fascinating as I found Hawksmoor's work, there was a more significant pattern, a bigger picture emerging.

What I found out shocked me and has taken years for me to process.

Chapter 4
False Brethren

It took me a long time to get my head around the politics of the era, to understand the context. I knew lots of dates and facts but didn't understand the big picture.

That all changed for me when I learnt about a sermon, called *The Perils of False Brethren,* given at St Paul's Cathedral on November 5th 1709, by a man called Henry Sacheverell. This sermon caused a political upheaval, is credited with swinging an election, and brought several unrelated facts together for me: it offers a brilliantly clear insight into the politics of the time.

The two political parties of the day were the Whigs and the Tories. The Whigs were very much the 'Lion' Party, invested in the City, trade and were the architects of Empire. The Tory faction was loyal to the Crown, the 'Unicorn' Stuart monarchy, favouring Divine Right, a landed aristocracy and things as they had always been.

The Whigs had been in Government since November 5th 1688. I need to pull that date apart a bit for the context to be clear.

Not *November 5th 1605*, when Guy Fawkes got caught trying to blow up Parliament.

Not *1588* when the Spanish Armada threatened England with invasion.

November 5th 1688 was when this country was last invaded and conquered, by William of Orange, who became William III of England and reigned with his wife Mary. William had timed his invasion to remind people he was a Protestant coming to save them from the Catholic threat. The arrival of William was the end of the last Stuart king, the Catholic James II, Mary's father, who was allowed to escape to France. It was also the end of a turbulent century of Stuart Kings, and their Tory supporters.

So when, on *November 5th 1688*, William III invaded he decided the fate of the nation. England would not be run by a Catholic-leaning, Divine Right monarch; the Stuart way. It would be run by a figure-head monarch of a trading Empire, modelled on Venice.

This put an end to hundreds of years of tradition, in which the rural economy dominated, and lord and serf lived separate lives. Instead more and more people came to the City, and lived by skill and trade.

In the City the old hierarchies fell apart. In the City subversive religious and political opinions flourished. In the City all a man needed was money and he could dress like an aristocrat, eat like an aristocrat, live like one, solely by applying his talent. Some found this idea positively offensive. Some still find it threatening today.

For over twenty years this Whig way of life had dominated the body politic. Following the death of William III and the Coronation of James II's other daughter, Queen Anne, in 1702, the Tories slowly made their way back into positions of power, having been turned out of office in 1688, the same time as James II.

On 5th November 1709, Henry Sacheverell gave the annual sermon to the City Fathers at St Paul's, celebrating the delivery of the King from the Catholic Gunpowder Plot. For twenty years the Whigs had used this national celebration to commemorate *both* November 5ths, both the Gunpowder Plot and William III's invasion, as deliverance from Catholic plotting and scheming.

But Sacheverell was a Tory, and had been given one of the most important sermons in the country. It would be read in all the nine thousand parish churches across the country. This was state media circa 1709, and he used it to devastating effect. Some feared his sermon would provoke another Civil War; others hoped that it would.

His sermon focussed on what he called *False Brethren*, the bad brotherhood that had caused the fanaticism of the Gunpowder Plot. But, worse than the Catholics fanatics, Sacheverell said, were the *False Brethren* who had killed the King, Charles I, in 1649. This was an unprecedented accusation.

Sacheverell said these *False Brethren* had led to civil war and dissent, their liberality in religion led to factionalism and strife, their looser ethics had led to the moral destruction of the nation. These *False Brethren*, Sacheverell said, were the cause of the deep malaise and collapse of the Natural Order that had led to the treacherous murder of Charles I. These *False Brethren*, by killing the King, had done more damage than the famous failure of the Gunpowder Plot.

You have to bear in mind who was in the audience that day at St Paul's Cathedral. Many of the City Fathers had supported Cromwell and Parliament and had helped finance the war against the King. They had also backed the invasion of William III, because, by and large, these men were traders, not land-owners. They had backed whomever seemed best placed to offer stability in commerce.

Sacheverell was calling them *False Brethren*. The City Fathers had, in a way, started the Civil War. When, on 4th January 1642, King Charles I had tried to pursue five Members of Parliament into the City, they had refused to hand them over and locked the City gates against him. Such open defiance of the King by the City forced Charles I to leave London about a week later. He set up his court in Oxford and the fighting began soon after.

Sacheverell was openly implying the City Fathers were guilty of treason. For the mob it became open season to ridicule the merchants and mercers. The City Fathers had been brought down a peg or two in front of the whole nation. People across the country quoted the sermon and showed their loyalty by accusing others of being *False Brethren*. No doubt many of the bankers went home and considered their travel arrangements, having changed their undergarments.

Sacheverell asserted "*the steady belief in the subject's obligation to absolute and unconditional Obedience to the Supreme Power in all things lawful, and the utter illegality of Resistance upon any pretence whatsoever*".

This is the Divine Right approach, every subject should obey the Crown just like every Christian obeys God: without question. He said the moral relativism of the *False Brethren* was a "*spurious and villainous notion, which will take in Jews, Quakers, Mahometans and anything, as well as Christians.*"

The *False Brethren* had turned a naturally obedient people against God and his representative on earth, the King.

The reaction to his Sermon was immediate: he was cheered by crowds in the City. This has the ring of a stage-managed event on a lot of levels.

What is clear is that Sacheverell had tapped into a popular feeling that the Nation had been riven by too many events, too many triumphs and tragedies, too much innovation and uncertainty, too much change.

In 1666 London had been through its Anus Mirabilis, had seen off Fire, Famine, War and Disease. This 'Year of Miracles' was interpreted by some as God's vengeance on the City for the death of Charles I.

In 1688 there had been an invasion and another upheaval in government. In 1709 people wanted peace and quiet, maybe a little solemnity, and the simple certainties of life to be re-established. Sacheverell's sermon is credited with turning the popular sentiment to the Tories, and as previously stated, they returned to power in 1710.

This restored hope to Hawksmoor, who had been left bitterly disappointed by the failure to rebuild London wholesale. His Churches were built and financed by the Tories' Commission for building fifty new Churches of 1711. The Tories were concerned that the City had grown out of control, and had become the home to dissenters, rebels and unorthodox religious sects.

The City's narrow, crooked streets created narrow, crooked and ungodly people; people all too liable to forget their *"duty to obey"*, as Sacheverell put it.

This Sermon clarified for me how these two rival groups, Whig and Tory, practised their politics in public. It also offers an insight into something more obscure and private, the phrase *False Breth*ren, it seems, had a meaning only some people would understand, it was code.

It was whilst I was walking around the grounds of Hawsmoor's Church St Anne's, in Limehouse, that I found something that put the sense of mystery around Hawksmoor into sharp focus. I realised if I was going to try to understand what he was doing there was somewhere I had to start, however reluctantly. In some sense this clue ended the mystery of why Hawksmoor did what he did.

The Pyramid

In the grounds of St Anne's in Limehouse stands a pyramid, about ten feet tall, made of five massive pieces of stone which create five layers laid on top of one another. The bottom two sections are plain, but on the third, protruding out from the surface, is the Royal Coat of Arms, now worn away by the weather.

Above this, on the fourth section, is engraved "The Wisdom of Solomon", barely visible from a distance. My stomach dropped and

47

my pulse quickened; I knew that this meant I was dealing with an infamously obscure organisation. Hawksmoor was a Freemason.

I knew that Freemasonry revered the Temple of Solomon at Jerusalem as some kind of ideal, mythic building. I knew Solomon was the central figure in their mythology. Hawksmoor was a mason, a real stone-cutter by training, he was interested in history and ancient cultures.

It suddenly dawned on me how obvious this was: Hawksmoor was a Freemason, part of that famously secretive tradition. I knew they still existed and had their headquarters near Covent Garden.

So, I called the Freemasons' Central Hall on Great Queen Street, and got an email address. When I asked about Hawksmoor, I was politely directed to Vaughan Hart's book, 'Nicholas Hawksmoor', chapter four, entitled 'Freemasonry and Hawksmoor's study of the Temple of Solomon'. I bought and read this book, and it was clear Hawksmoor was deeply inspired by masonic ideas.

The Pyramid stands as a permanent reminder, silently screaming out its message to those who are willing to listen. The most striking thing to me was the way the protruding Royal Crest on the third section was under the subtly carved 'Wisdom of Solomon' in the fourth section. Symbolically the message was clear. The Wisdom of Solomon stood above Royalty, was closer to God.

Looking back, it was pretty obvious that Hawksmoor was a Freemason. It had become fashionable to hang out with the Masons like Hawksmoor who were rebuilding London; that's how London Freemasonry began. Or so the story goes.

The roots of Freemasonry are actually much more tangled than the official story suggests. The historian Elias Ashmole wrote about it in the 1640s. It seems to have flourished underground, or at least mostly unrecorded in the later part of the 1600s. Ashmole like many others was loyal to the Stuart Crown during the Civil war.

On delving deeper it became clear that a *certain kind* of Freemasonry had become fashionable in a very elite circle in the Court of James I. James had come down from Scotland and been eulogised as a 'New Solomon', a king of deep wisdom and almost divine judgment. James

I's son, Charles I, had used initiation into this mystical Freemasonry as a recruiting tool and reward for loyalty during the Civil War.

These secret connections remained important, especially after Charles I's execution in 1649. These Freemasons were at the heart of the attempts to restore the Stuart family to the throne. Many rich and powerful families identified secretly as 'Jacobites', loyal to the Stuart family even after 1688. It was always a bit of a mystery to me how such utter failures as kings had commanded such deep love and loyalty from their followers. It seems that the Stuarts used their form of Freemasonry to bind people to them. This is 'Scottish' Freemasonry.

On further investigation however, Freemasonry was not just 'Scottish', but also 'Irish'. This distinction was about as significant as the difference between Protestant and Catholic[12]. To the outsider they are all Christians, as some might say all Freemasons are the same, but to the people involved that was not the case. They experienced very different realities, realities that reflected their secret beliefs.

The 'Scottish' masonry looked to the Temple in Jerusalem for inspiration, but the 'Irish' version of the craft claimed associations with Egypt.

Ireland has an ancient association with Egypt, dating back at least to the 4th Century Monastic Tradition of the Coptic Church. Based in Egypt, this form of Christianity had sent out missionaries long before Rome. This 'Celtic' or Irish Christianity predated the arrival of Roman missionaries and was organised like the Coptic Church, for example; they had no Bishops and favoured monasteries over churches.

The origin of Christianity in Britain is a very interesting subject, too big to be covered here in any detail. It is probably more accurate to call this early Christianity 'British', rather than 'Irish' but Freemasonry distinguished between the Scottish and Irish traditions, and for clarity I'm going to stick with those labels.

The 'Irish' tradition of masonry was Egyptian-influenced, spiritual and embedded in a 'Christian' tradition. Its roots are buried too deep for us to trace here but it was this 'Irish' tradition of Freemasonry that Hawksmoor believed had built Stonehenge and later the Gothic Cathedrals.

So, when the Scottish First Grand Lodge convened in 1717, the official beginning of the organisation that still exists today, it had a rival with a proud heritage. The antagonism between 'Scottish' and 'Irish' Freemasonry was eventually settled in 1813 when the Duke of Sussex became the head of both orders, creating the United Grand Lodge.

The differences between these two factions were not trivial. For example, during the American War of Independence, 'Scottish' masons were generally loyal to the Crown, whilst the 'Irish' seemed to favour the Revolution. Some in the City sent money and supplies to their 'Irish', revolutionary brethren, supporting them against the Crown and openly celebrated the establishment of the Republic.

But in Hawksmoor's time these differences were still working themselves out, under the surface of society. They lend a layer of meaning to Sacheverell's notion of *False Brethren*. It seems clear at least some of these *False Brethren* were Freemasons from a rival order.

There was conflict on the surface between Whigs and Tories, but the machinations of power that lay beneath are difficult to discern except in the broadest terms. The Scottish Masons favoured the Stuarts, Divine Right style kingship, and were Tories. The Irish Fraternity leant toward the property rights, limited Democracy and figurehead Monarchs like William III and were Whigs.

With this broader context in mind, I began to see events more clearly. I understood the 'Lions' and 'Unicorns' were rival factions with differing politics, based on their respective religious outlooks. These had public and private aspects, were deeply held, and mutually exclusive. Only one side could win: Britain would either become a trading empire, or remain an agrarian aristocracy. It's obvious who won, but what amazed me is how dirty the fight became.

We can now turn to the Restoration of Charles II in 1660, and examine events in terms of this rivalry.

King of the Hill

The Tory out-look entailed a 'natural order' and at the head of that order was the King. Understanding this belief system is integral to understanding the times.

Tories like Hawksmoor believed subjects had an absolute duty to obey God's anointed representative on earth and nothing could absolve a subject from that duty. This notion of a god-appointed absolute and infallible king was introduced, and tested to destruction, by the vain and venal Stuarts. They asserted their Divine Right to rule, but exercised it like crass, selfish children.

This caused the Tory supporters of Divine Right considerable difficulties. In their world-view the Civil War had been not just illegal, it was ungodly, it was the product of corrupted and evil souls, it was the work of the devil. It was the work of the righteous to see this evil defeated. The *False Brethren* in the country must be rooted out.

It is hard to imagine today, but this battle was not just political, not just financial, not just religious. It was *cosmological*, everything was at stake, even God himself was in jeopardy.

In the form of King Charles I (1600-1649), God had been killed. The status of Charles I as the only Martyr of the Anglican Church is hard to over-emphasize. Royalists still fast on 30th January every year to commemorate Charles' execution. I'm sure, as a loyal Tory, Hawksmoor would have observed this fast.

Even after he had been defeated, Charles I still exerted an extra-ordinary influence on those about him.

While the Civil War was still being fought Cromwell sent Charles to the Isle of Wight, where he stayed as a guest of the local gentry. This included the family of the scientist Robert Hooke (1635-1703), who later became integral to the success of the Royal Society.

The kind of loyalty Charles I could command in others was almost unbelievable, and one example of this is particularly relevant to this story.

John Hooke, Robert's father, was minor gentry on the Isle of Wight, and a committed Tory. He did everything he could to support Charles, risking personal ruin and arrest in the process.

On September 23rd 1648, John Hooke drew up his last will and testament, although he was not ill and showed no sign of sickness. A couple of weeks later he was dead, and though the cause of death is not recorded Lisa Jardine in her biography of Hooke, indicates she believes it was suicide. [13]

She says, "Robert Hooke's father's death may have been linked directly to the King's fading fortunes [14]. It seems John Hooke may have over-reached himself financially, or perhaps was in danger of being fined or imprisoned for the assistance he gave Charles. He took the way out that enabled his family to inherit whatever he had left.

Robert Hooke would have been 13. In his father's will he was left with £40, a chest and all the family's books.

A few days before or after his father's suicide Robert was taken to London, where he was apprenticed to the Dutch painter, and ardent Royalist, Peter Lely. Hooke's education was provided by the headmaster of Westminster School, who was called Dr Busby. It seems his future was put in the hands of a group of loyal royal supporters[15].

At the time, committing suicide was seen as a mortal sin which would have condemned John Hooke's soul to hell for eternity. Robert Hooke became an ardent royalist and played a significant role in London at the time of the Great Fire. He never forgave those who he believed had caused his father's death.

Robert Hooke's scientific work is much less well known that it should be. Did you know that it was he, not Newton, who first proposed the inverse square law to describe Gravity?[15] Newton now gets all the credit.

For reasons that will become clearer Hooke's Tory legacy was deliberately hidden and his reputation destroyed by Whig historians. Hooke, like Hawksmoor, was on the losing side.

Brothers in Arms

After their father's execution by Cromwell, the Stuart brothers, Charles, later Charles II, and James, later James II, had become the great hope of Tory England.

They fought on after their father's death, had been routinely defeated and eventually escaped to France. In 1651, Charles' arrival was described by the Venetian Ambassador to Paris. It's worth reading in full,

The king of England entered Paris on Wednesday evening, being met by the Duke of Orleans, the queen his mother, the Duke of York and many grandees of the Court as well.

His suite consisted of a gentleman and a lackey. His dress was more calculated to move laughter than respect, and his aspect is so changed that those who were nearest believed him to be one of the lower servants.

He relates that after the battle, he escaped with a gentleman and a soldier, who had spent most of his days in highway robbery and had a great experience of hidden paths. Thus accompanied the king travelled by night, always on foot, as far as the remote parts of Scotland, but finding no means for embarking or place of safety, he had himself shaven, as a more complete disguise, and decided to return to England.

There by ill fortune he was recognised by a miller, who began to shout to raise the country.

Though destitute of the royal trappings, he did not lack prudence and courage to extricate himself from such a perilous adventure, as he hurried into a neighbouring wood, where he hid among the branches of a tree.

In spite of the number and energy of the countrymen they never thought of raising their eyes, although the wood was full of men looking for him. When night came he took the way to London, where he arrived without being recognised and remained there in the same disguise.

He was lodged in the house of a woman who got a ship for him, and to avoid risks in going through the city, he wore her clothes, and with a bag of washing on his head he got to his ship in safety and so crossed.

Paris, the 7th November, 1651[17].

Charles Stuart, who would return to be crowned as Charles II, left this country disguised as a washerwoman. I can only imagine the emotions this evoked in God's appointed ruler.

He was, apparently, in the habit of looking himself in the mirror and remarking, *"Oddsfish but I am ugly"*, *Oddsfish* being an abbreviation of *'God's flesh'.* He saw himself as God, and God was ugly. Who'd be a king?!

It's fair to say the Stuart brothers were more than a little disturbed by their experiences, they were angry.

It wasn't just their father had been killed, that they had been humiliated on the battlefield, nor was it just about their loss of wealth and status. They believed they were like gods, and the City mob had killed god-on-earth, their father, satanically usurping the Natural Order. Revenge was their duty.

The Stuart brothers lived as guests of their cousin, King Louis XIV of France, the most powerful ruler in Europe at the time. They were family, and dynasty mattered more than nation.

The Stuart brothers tolerated the English generally but they wholeheartedly, passionately and definitely despised the City mob. They shared their disgust of the urban rabble with their cousin and looked around in envy at the Paris the architect Bernini was building for him. A Capital City worthy of the *Sun-King*.

At his coronation in 1660 Charles II swore to be a good Protestant, on his death-bed, however, he converted back to Catholicism, a true measure of the man.

He was charismatic and affable, he was also a consummate liar and manipulator. He appears to have believed in very little. He had numerous mistresses, giving him at least 14 illegitimate children. His court was known for a kind of amoral nihilism and, not surprisingly, hedonism.

Charles II had promised Louis XIV to bring Britain back to Catholicism. He twice brought England to War against the Dutch at Louis' request, pitting the two Protestant Naval powers against each other, leaving the French free to fight the Dutch on land.

Charles lobbied parliament for funds to wage war while taking secret payments from his cousin Louis too[18].

When he returned to London to be crowned, Charles saw the same mob that had killed his father celebrating his restoration, he is reported to have said something like: *"We should have come back sooner..."*. If nothing else, in his years in exile he had cultivated a kind of gallows wit.

King Charles II in full regalia

**Charlie the washerwoman fleeing the
country and looking a little less dignified.**

A few of the great and the good, like Cowley, had gone into exile with the Stuart brothers in France. This is when the ultra-loyal Home Guard, originally called the King's Guard, was established. They protect the Crown to this day.

Charles II's friends included the poet and essayist Abraham Cowley.

Cowley had spied for the Stuarts and written witty poems about how great they were. He was also the first person to write about cocaine in English, celebrating coca's virtues in verse, and no doubt they all enjoyed them too[19]. So began the recorded relationship between rich Englishmen and Columbian snow.

One favourite in Charles II's Court, Lord Sedley, is worth a mention here. He was fined £500, a fortune in those days, for his public behaviour.

He had appeared, in broad daylight, naked on the balcony of the Cock Inn overlooking Bow Street where he began to enact "*all the postures of lust and buggery that could be imagined*", continued by "*abusing the scripture*", delivering a mock sermon in which he declared "*he hath to sell such a powder as should make all the cunts in town run after him*".

The onlookers then witnessed as "*he took a glass of wine and washed his prick in it... and drank the King's health*".

His finale was to "*excrementize*" over the crowd beneath him. Charles II lent him the money to pay his fine after Sedley complained "*he thought he was the first man that paid for shitting*"[20].

I think it's pretty clear the 'powder' Lord Sedley was referring to was not nutmeg. Charles II's court became synonymous with debauchery.

The Earl of Rochester coined a couplet that became famous,

> "*Restless he rolls, from whore to whore,*
> *A merry monarch, scandalous and poor*".

Sedley in full flow

Other, less flattering, descriptions were made. Charles II frustrated the ambitions of those who worked for the Crown, he would not take his office seriously and, except when it came to money, he had very little interest in government.

His Lord Chancellor, Edward Hyde (Lord Clarendon) said Charles attitude made him 'despair of his life'. Rather deal with the serious matters of the day, Charles preferred the traditional gentlemanly pursuits of hunting and frolicking with milk-maids.

Abraham Cowley wrote,
>*"God the first garden made, and the first city Cain".*

So the city was, in Cowley's *royally-sanctioned* opinion, artificial, diabolical and, perhaps, needed to be taught a lesson. Cain had killed Abel out of envy.

The Great Plague of 1665 and Great Fire of 1666 were interpreted by some as acts of God, as divine punishment for the death of Charles I. Charles II's opinion on this theory is not recorded.

Believing in very little, wit was the currency in his court. He was cynical and aloof and, I suggest, would have little affection for the City that had humiliated his family and executed his father.

That he spoke with his childhood friend Sir Christopher Wren about such matters is reasonable. As we'll see, Wren drew up street plans for rebuilding London *unbelievably* quickly. Wren's father was Dean of St George's Chapel Windsor and, as such, he administered the Order of the Garter, the most prestigious honour in the country.

Christopher Wren's father was a close confidant of Charles I. Wren's uncle was a bishop who was imprisoned by Cromwell for his Royalist sympathies. Wren was two tears younger than Charles II, they had grown up in close proximity. It is still considered controversial by some to say they knew and played together as boys. Between them as men they drew up plans for London as the Capital of an Empire.

Turning up the Heat

Charles and his brother James, Abraham Cowley, Sir Christopher Wren and Robert Hooke were Hawksmoor's people.

They were all his seniors in age as well as in status. In Hawksmoor there was a man who could help bridge the gap between working stone masons, some of whom belonged to the 'Irish' tradition of Freemasonry, and the fashionable, speculative 'Scottish' Freemasons of the Royal Court.

It seems inconceivable he wasn't there, with Wren, at the Goose and Grid Iron Pub on June 24th 1717, when Freemasonry officially began.

Reading what Hawksmoor said about the rebuilding of London had really stuck with me. He and his friends were not just disappointed, but angry that the opportunity to rebuild from scratch hadn't happened. This anger and disappointment was a popular gripe, a trope, among them.

About this time I came across Adrian Gilbert's book *New Jerusalem*, which details the machinations of a group he labels *Rosicrucian*, and their involvement with the redesign of London, even before the Fire had happened.

I also saw a documentary about the Fire on Channel 4 that included the author Adrian Tinneswood. What he said in this documentary really got me thinking. He mentioned witness reports of James II rescuing people.

On further investigation it became clear Tinneswood was quoting from a parliamentary report on the fire:

"A true and faithful account of the several informations exhibited to the hounourable committee appointed by the Parliament to inquire into the late dreadful burning of the city of London together with other informations touching the insolency of popish priests and Jesuites ..."[21]

When I first read this report I couldn't believe what I was seeing. Documentary evidence, from Parliament, that *they* saw Catholics as responsible for the fire. I couldn't dismiss this as idle gossip or conspiracy theory if Parliament had bothered to investigate.

Very much like when I first saw Shakespeare's signatures, I couldn't process what it meant.

I had to go to the National Archives at Kew to look at it, what I read I found initially impossible to understand. On reflection some of this report is clearly biased, clearly anti-Catholic in its intent. But there was one aspect of the story that made no sense to me; I didn't understand the context at the time.

One thing several different witnesses agreed on was the role of James, Duke of York, later King James II, in rescuing arsonists. People who had been caught committing arson were rescued from the civil authorities by the King's brother.

This report was obviously controversial at the time, some members of the committee repudiated its findings, others were steadfast in support.

Many people maintained that James was complicit in the fire for their entire lives, this included one John Tillotson, who later became Archbishop of Canterbury[22]. So this opinion was not one found only at the lunatic fringe, very 'respectable' people maintained the fire was deliberate.

I left Kew with a head-ache and a knot in my stomach. This information shattered my understanding of what I had read up until that point. Slowly, thinking through Tinneswood's words on that TV documentary, and reframing events Adrian Gilbert called Rosicrucian, the kaleidoscope of events in 1660's London began to fall into place.

According to Hawksmoor, *"when they had so favourable an opportunity to rebuild London, the most august town in the world, ought for the public good to have guided it into regular and commodious form, and not to have suffered it to run into an ugly inconvenient self destroying unwieldy monster"*[23].

The last phrase is so dense that I run out of breath trying to say it: his exasperation lives on in his choice of words. And he was not alone. Reading around and about this period of English history over the years something has happened in my mind's eye. So many accidents and random events seem to conspire that it became difficult to see them as unrelated.

There comes a point when the straws of coincidence break the back of the camel of causation(!) Here comes the Actuarial bit, see how the odds stack up.

The London Monument
Based on a drawing by Sutton Nicholls 1753

Chapter 5
The Four Unicorns of the Apocalypse
Fire, War, Disease and Famine

FIRE

Every child in England learns that in 1666 a fire started on a Saturday night in a Baker's Shop on Pudding Lane, accidentally burning down the City.

What is weird about reading accounts from the time is that no one in London believed that.

Edward Hyde, The Lord Chancellor, reported to the King that by the Monday, while the fire was still raging, there was a *"universal conclusion, that this fire came not by chance"* [24].

Everyone agreed it was deliberate.

Before I had read what Hyde said, I'd seen an inscription on Wren and Hooke's massive Monument to the Fire. On the base of that massive stone pillar is an inscription in Latin, still visible today.

In translation it says...

In the year of Christ 1666, on the 2nd September, at a distance eastward from this place of 202 feet, which is the height of this column, a fire broke out in the dead of night, which, the wind blowing devoured even distant buildings, and rushed devastating through every quarter with astonishing swiftness and noise.

It consumed 89 churches, gates, the Guildhall, public edifices, hospitals, schools, libraries, a great number of blocks of buildings, 13,200 houses, 400 streets.

Of the 26 wards, it utterly destroyed 15, and left 8 mutilated and half-burnt.

The ashes of the City, covering as many as 436 acres, extended on one side from the Tower along the bank of the Thames to the church of the Templars, on the other side from the north-east along the walls to the head of Fleet-ditch. Merciless to the wealth and estates of the citizens, it was harmless to their lives, so as throughout to remind us of the final destruction of the world by fire.

The havoc was swift. A little space of time saw the same city most prosperous and no longer in being.

On the third day, when it had now altogether vanquished all human counsel and resource, at the bidding, as we may well believe of heaven, the fatal fire stayed its course and everywhere died out.

But Popish frenzy, which wrought such horrors, is not yet quenched.

The last sentence was added in 1681 and then removed in 1830. Read it again.

In 1681 the official monument to the Great Fire blamed Catholics for starting it, this accusation - carved in stone – was later removed.

The official version of the Great Fire changed.

How and why had that happened?

How is it we are never taught at school that the *"universal conclusion"* of Londoners at the time was the fire was not an accident?

How was it that this *"Popish frenzy"* of fanatical Catholicism, blamed for starting the fire, had been quietly removed from history?

The vilification of Catholicism, especially since the Gunpowder plot of 1605, had become state policy. Catholics lived under draconian laws restricting their movement, their ability to practise certain professions: their beliefs were taxed.

This policy pre-dated the Stuarts who, as discussed, were not enthusiastic about it, but events kept Catholic 'fanaticism' in the forefront of national conversation.

In these circumstances it would be easy to understand if Londoners had believed Catholics were behind the Fire.

Funny thing was, they didn't believe that either. The prevailing conspiracy theory at the time of the Fire was that the Dutch, their fellow Protestants, had started it. To understand this we need to step back from the Fire and look at the War.

WAR

The First Anglo-Dutch War (1652-54), was waged under Cromwell.

The dynamic was basically either London or Amsterdam would become the new Venice, and dominate global trade. The question was which, for the bankers, was the better bet. It all rested on the ability to command the sea.

Cromwell's reforms had set the English Navy on the course for world domination. He combatted corruption and promoted on merit, applied science to the design of ships and their weaponry. The decades of nepotism, cronyism and keeping it in the family were over. The effects were revolutionary. Within ten years the English Navy became the best in the world, an advantage that even the Royal Navy, led by James Stuart after the Restoration in 1660, couldn't squander. But it got very close.

The Second (1665-67) and Third (1672-74) Anglo-Dutch Wars were both disastrous for England, nearly destroying trade and crippling the urban economy. Both wars were started by the actions of the same man, the Stuart brothers' long-term friend, Captain Robert Holmes.

Captain Holmes, like Abraham Cowley, was one of the elite group of Royalists who had joined the Stuart Brothers in their French exile. As such it is not surprising he was instrumental in fulfilling Charles II's obligation to his cousin, Louis XIV of France, to start a war with the Dutch.

In 1664, Holmes sailed a flotilla of ships, belonging to James' Royal African Company, to Guinea, where, so the story went, there was a mountain of gold.

Perhaps unsurprisingly that mountain never appeared, but Holmes persuaded the crew he had tricked onto the voyage they may as well engage the nearby Dutch settlements and take their fortresses. This incident instigated the Second Anglo-Dutch War, and the prize for the victor was domination of the spice trade.

Spices were desirable and profitable but one spice in particular was an absolute necessity for those in the know. To understand this we need to step back from the War and look at a Disease.

DISEASE

The Bubonic Plague had decimated Europe, infamously, in the 14th century, and in sporadic pockets ever since.

It had killed millions over the centuries. Outbreaks were still common, especially among the poor.

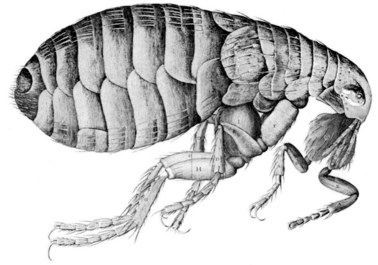

Plague carrier and detester of Nutmeg
The flea as drawn by Robert Hooke – 1665

Of all the medicines then known, nutmeg was the only effective defence against *the Plague*. The same chemical mixture that makes nutmeg slightly psychoactive, also makes fleas flee, insects hate it. Nutmeg does, irrefutably, offer you effective immunity to plague because the fleas won't bite you[25].

Since the middle ages the Venetians had bought the spice from Arab traders, but had not been able to locate its source.

Its effects were known, it warded off the disease, hence it became incredibly desirable, and the most profitable cargo in the world.

This information was not shared universally, however, as if the general populace had known the about nutmeg's ability to ward off plague, its price would have been even higher.

In 1511 the Portuguese had identified nutmeg's source in the islands of Indonesia. Not long after, the Dutch came along and took control gaining a monopoly that lasted until the English, under Cromwell, had settled an island nearby.

The treaty that ended the Second War in 1667 included England giving up its spice island, swapping it for Manhattan, which the Dutch had called New Amsterdam, but James Stuart renamed New York, after himself, as Duke of York.

Some people today laugh that the Dutch gave up New York for nutmeg, but that's because we never see anyone die of bubonic plague anymore.

Later, on 23 March 1672, having been demoted, vilified and then restored to office by James, now in command of his own squadron of ships in Portsmouth, Holmes launched an unprovoked attack on the Dutch Smyrna convoy, which was known for its exotic, expensive cargo. This started the Third Anglo-Dutch War.

So it is fair to say Robert Holmes had form. He didn't like the Dutch, and, I dare say, they didn't like him.

This antagonism between the English and Dutch, which was nurtured by Louis XIV over the control of trade generally, and nutmeg in particular, resulted in many casualties on both sides.

Returning to the year of the Fire, perhaps the most famous event of the Second Anglo-Dutch War was what became known as Holmes' Bonfire.

Holmes' Bonfire

On 19th August 1666, Holmes attacked a Dutch Port, destroyed 140 merchant vessels and set fire to the town of West-Terschelling, killing about a hundred people.

It was a devastating and destructive raid on a soft, sitting target.

The Dutch were outraged at an attack on the civilian town, but back in England Holmes was a hero. With this attack still on Londoners' minds, the Second War with the Dutch was all the news when the Fire started.

Charles II had started the War with the Dutch and driven a wedge between the two Protestant Naval powers that enabled the French to press more vigorously on land.

To repeat something that's hard to believe but is uncontested history: Charles agreed to convert England back to Catholicism and took money from Louis as often as he could[26].

The Stuarts' Dutch Wars were part geopolitical and religious manoeuvring; part profiteering.

As the Fire raged the story went about that Dutchmen, in revenge for Holmes' Bonfire, had been seen setting fire to their houses.

Some said it was a Dutchman who owned the Baker's shop on Pudding Lane where the Fire had started. In what was already a pretty xenophobic city it soon became dangerous for foreigners on the streets, people with accents became the victims of frenzy.

Amidst the smoke and flames some foreigners were beaten, mutilated and killed.

London was, at that time, a tinder-box waiting to ignite.

The year 1666 had long fascinated the superstitious, with all kinds of prophecies and prognostications being made. For example many found deep significance in the fact 1666, in roman numerals, uses every numerical sign: MDCLXVI. These artefacts of the imagination were, it seems, given Royal sanction.

Samuel Pepys reports that the Stuart brothers referred to the predictions made by *Mother Shipton* about London burning. Mother Shipton was a *prophetess* who'd died over a hundred years previously. Ever since people had been putting words into her mouth and she became a popular figure on the penny-sheets, which were about as reliable as Fox News.

That the Stuarts referred to Mother Shipton is remarkable because they were appealing to the popular mind, something they didn't do often.

For Pepys to have mentioned this meant this was meant to be a matter of record: the Stuarts said they believed London was cursed, as set out by *Mother Shipton*.

In the run up to 1666 this kind of story may well have been put about to soften people up psychologically before the main event.

Indeed, during the fire, doom-mongers were found everywhere, claiming the Fire was God's judgement, that London was Babylon and Babylon must burn.

It seems some people were so busy telling everyone else, "I told you this was going to happen", that they forgot to help put the fire out, they enjoyed the carnage.

The previous year, at least 100,000 people in London, all too poor to buy nutmeg, had died of the Plague. The Poet John Dryden called it *Annus Mirabilis*, Year of Miracles. It was all too much for some people. They turned to God to explain the inexplicable.

The politician Sir Nathaniel Hobart said "*the image of this terrible judgement has made such an impression in the souls of every one of us, that it will not be effaced while we live*".

In Parliament it was described as "*the Justice of God*" and "*the Wrath of God*"[27].

Samuel Pepys suffered from what we now call post-traumatic stress and couldn't sleep well for months, being plagued by dreams of fire.

> "*War, plague and fire, against us all conspire,*
> *We the war, God the plague, but who raised the fire?*"
> Andrew Marvell, M.P. - 'The Third Advice to a Painter', 1667.

Again and again you read the same sort of thing, this from someone who was a member of Parliament and metaphysical poet.

Who raised the fire?!

People at the time were sure about it, the Fire had not been an accident. The rumour that Dutchmen had started was superseded by events. It is possible Charles and James had wanted to use this Dutch narrative to deepen the divide between England and Holland, it would have suited their long-term plans. But there was little supporting evidence, and what evidence there is points to the arsonists having Royal connections.

Matchmaking

A whole library of books has been written about the Fire. What follows is a brief run through of selected events, that is not meant to be exhaustive or definitive, just, I hope, interesting. Cumulatively they critically undermine our official history:

June 1561
The spire of Old St Paul's Cathedral collapsed and the building had been in need of repair since then. Wren had been involved with the old cathedral since 1661.

1663
Wren returned from Paris where he had seen what the architect Bernini had been doing for Louis XIV.

August 1666
In the spring Wren drew up his first design for a dome for St Paul's. It was accepted, in principle, on 27th August. A scaffold is erected and barrels of tar are applied to the leaking roof.

Saturday, 1st September
John Graunt, statistician, is a newly appointed trustee of the New River Company. The New River Company had created a canal that diverted river water into a reservoir in Islington.

This artificial supply of water was critical to the health and well-being of Londoners. John Graunt turns off the water supply, locks the door and disappears taking the keys with him. This is unprecedented[28].

Thomas Farriner, baker of Pudding Lane, puts out his oven-fire, and, at about 10pm places new fuel in the oven, ready for the morning. He's done this for over twenty years without an incident.

Sunday 2nd September
About 1am a fire breaks out in Farriner's bakery. It is a brick-lined work-shop designed and built to handle heat.

The fire and smoke are so incredibly intense that Farriner, his daughter and apprentice all have to climb out a first story window and across into a neighbour's bedroom.

Farriner looks on in shock, trying to understand what in his bakery could burn so hot. He immediately cries foul, there's no way, he says, his bakery could burn so fiercely. Flour in his bakery might have exploded, but this did not happen, the fire was intense and sustained.

There is no immediate panic, however; fires are common and there are traditional procedures to follow. Every Parish church has hooks and ladders to help pull down buildings to help contain the fire, but the tools in St Magnus the Martyr are old and hardly fit for purpose, so the Fire grows.

At night a breeze tends to blow up the hill from the river. Pudding Lane is known for this. It has been a hot and dry summer, so the Fire grows.

There is a problem with the local water supply and so loose chains of people pass buckets of water up from the Thames, but to little effect, so the Fire grows. The awareness that somehow the water supply isn't working begins to foster a sense of panic.

The City's Fire Engines are simple pumping machines of enormous size and weight, that cannot gain access through the narrow Pudding Lane, so the Fire grows.

Thomas Middleton, a Naval Surgeon, watches for two or three hours up a church steeple, near where Mansion House Tube is today.

Just a few hundred yards from Pudding Lane, he reported seeing fires breaking out in houses far from Farriner's Bakery.

The spire of St Laurence Pountney, a church over 100 yards away, all at once flares up like a candle. He later told the Parliamentary Committee, "*These and such like observations begat in me a persuasion that the fire was maintained by design*"[14].

He was not alone, there are dozens of similar reports. Were they all wrong? Or, maybe, our history teachers have taught us wrong?

The contrast between the official version and that of witnesses like Thomas Middleton is stark. It is not credible to dismiss witness reports because it doesn't fit with what you were told when you were five.

The Fire grows all night as warehouses by the river *spontaneously combust.*   These soon spread west down the north bank of the Thames. The Fire has a life of its own jumping between buildings hundreds of yards apart.

All the while a bemused Farriner cannot understand how a fire so intense started in his shop, he is in shock, can't believe his eyes. There was no way, he said, the contents of his bakery could burn so hot.

Sir Thomas Bloodworth, the Lord Mayor of London, visits the Fire in the afternoon and famously remarks, *"A woman could piss it out."*

He refuses to muster the City's resources and goes home, so the Fire grows.

Monday 3rd September
The Fire's insatiable and inexplicable growth confounds people and they look for someone to blame.

The rumour is spread that it's the Dutch, there are numerous people telling the same story - perhaps this rumour is actually prepared propaganda. Others see the fire in Biblical terms.

As the insanity spreads, anyone foreign or different or unknown is suspect. There is a climate of fear and despondency. On this day the people of London give up fighting the fire.

Samuel Pepys' diary records he went to Westminster and told the Stuart brothers about the fire. He says they seemed surprised.

It is worth pointing out that Pepys was very, very close to the Stuarts, and his account should be seen in that light. Pepys says the brothers demanded he seek out Bloodworth and set him to task.

Pepys found Bloodworth that afternoon; the Mayor complained he was frustrated as no one was listening to him, so he went home.

The man responsible for the City apparently leaves the Fire to its own devices. I find it hard to believe that the Lord Mayor of London was that big a fool.

Meanwhile Thomas Middleton, the Surgeon, was in Watling Street when a young man was thrown out of a tobacconist's shop. On inspection the man has gunpowder on him, has a French accent and lies, claiming the tobacconist knows him.

Middleton, with a Parish Constable takes the anonymous suspect to Old Bridewell correction house. The next day it burns down and no body is found. It is likely the suspect was taken to James' apartments in Whitehall, as were many others.

James Stuart and the King's *Life-Guards* ride round the City and assist those accused by the mob of arson, bringing them back to Whitehall Palace in Westminster. There are dozens of different eye witnesses to this. In the Parliamentary report on the Fire, you find their testimony saying the same thing: James rescued people caught committing arson and took them back to Whitehall palace.

The Parliamentary Report, *"A True and Faithfull Account..."*, is now available online. It was seeing Adrian Tinneswood quote witness statements from this report, saying James has rescued several people who had been caught in the act of arson, that really confirmed for me that there was more to this incident than we are taught.

It is not a fun or definitive read – but the various and consistent witness testimonies are impossible to ignore.

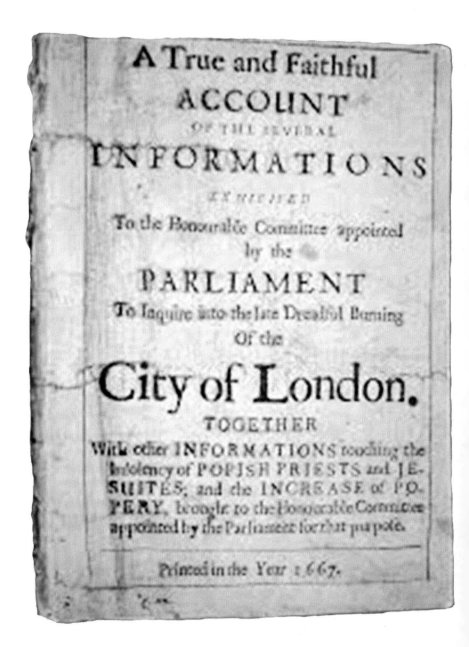

Witnesses

These examples are taken directly from that report:

Doctor John Packer informs, That he saw a Person in the time of the Fire, throw some combustible matter into a Shop in the Old Bayley, which he thinks was the Shop of an Apothecary; and that immediately thereupon he saw a great smoak, and smelt a smell of Brimstone. The Person that did this, immediately ran away; but upon the out-cry of the People he was taken by the Guards.

Mr. Randal, Mr. Haslem, and Mr. Humphry Bowyer, do all agree, That they saw a person flinging something into a House near St. Antholines Church; and that thereupon the House was on fire, and the smoak thereof infested the adjacent Houses. And when this was done, there was No fire near the place.

Mr. Michael March, an Officer in the Trained Bands in a Company of Sir Richard Browns, apprehended a Walloon in the time of the Fire, at the Nags-Head in Leaden-hall-Street, with an Instrument like a dark Lanthorn, made (as is conceived) to lay a Train of Powder, and it was filled with Gun-powder. There were two more of the same Nation in his company. They being asked to what use they employed the same Instrument, would give no Account thereof.

That near West-Smithfield in Cheek-Lane, there was a man taken in the very Act of firing a House, by the Inhabitants and Neighbours; and carrying him away through Smithfield, to have him before a Justice for the fact committed, The Kings Life-Guard perceiving it, made up unto them, and demanded their Prisoner from them; but they refused to let him go. The Life-Guard men told them, That he was one of the Kings Servants, and said, We will have him; and thereupon they drew out their Swords and Pistols, and rescued him out of the peoples hands by force of Arms.

In the time of the Fire, a Constable took a Frenchman firing a House, seized on him, and going to a Magistrate with him, met His Royal Highness the Duke of York, who asked the reason of the tumult: One told him that a Frenchman was taken firing a House; his Highness called for the man, who speak to him in French. The Duke asked, Who would attest it? The Constable said, I took him in the Act, and I will attest it. The Duke took him into his custody, and said, I will secure him. But he was heard of no more.

*On Monday the third of September, there was a Frenchman taken firing a House; and upon searching of him, Fire-Balls were found about him. At which time four of the Life-Guard rescued the Frenchman, and took him away from the People, **after their usual manner in the whole time of the Fire**. (Original emphasis)*[30]

The report explicitly states the King's 'Life Guards' were systematically protecting arsonists. These were the same men who had accompanied the Stuart brothers in France, their ultra-loyal supporters, who would later be renamed the Home Guard.

Having read these and other extracts I left Kew and tried not to think about it for a few days. That wasn't easy – everything I had read contradicted the official history, but there it was, in black and white.

To be fair, much of the report is given over to hearsay and gossip. Some of the report describes how Catholics were trying to convert Protestants: feelings were running very high and it seems the Committee had made up its mind who was to blame before they even sat down.

This is hardly unprecedented, and it does throw some of the findings of the report into doubt.

What cannot be denied, however, is the volume of independent sources, who would have hardly had time to collaborate on fake stories, all describing similar behaviour.

Would members of Parliament conspire to create false testimony that the Duke of York was rescuing arsonists?

That would be a very brave thing for anyone to do, and why would you bother, who would believe such an incredible story?

It seems to me politicians are not that heroic, or stupid, they would not have concocted a story that could get them hanged.

Is it possible that other anti-royal, anti-Catholic forces concocted the testimony of people like Thomas Middleton?

That seems to be the only other explanation for what the people say they saw the Duke of York do.

Most damning, of course, is that all this is not even mentioned in orthodox histories of the era, the facts are deliberately ignored and history of this incident hidden. It's all a bit too embarrassing for the future King to have conspired against his own Capital.

The report also makes clear that Southwark, on the other side of the river and up-wind of Pudding Lane, also burnt. This must have been arson.

During the inferno James had set up 'fire stations' across the City, each with a militia led by knights. Their job was to create fire-breaks by pulling down buildings in front of the fire, to rob it of fuel. These stations consume a lot of resources but proved completely ineffective.

The Life-Guards did successfully rescue a few arsonists, and the fire-stations were probably a deliberate distraction.

Tuesday 4th September
Overnight the Fire roared up Cheapside and encircled the Old St Paul's Cathedral.

Book-sellers had hidden their goods inside the enormous church for safety. An estimated £250,000 – about £50million in today's money – worth of reading material went up in flames as burning scaffolding and tar poured in through the southern side of the Cathedral roof.

This had something to do with Wren's repair work.

Within two hours this massive pile of thousands of tons of stone, much bigger than the present St Paul's, is reduced to rubble. Witnesses are left bemused how such a structure could disintegrate so quickly. Heat in excess of 1000 degrees caused iron to melt and the lead roofing to flow downhill to Ludgate. Wren's scaffolding and tar would have certainly contributed to this inferno.

The Fire jumps over James' fire stations, and the Fleet river; areas to the East and West of him are ablaze and he retreats.

One John Stewart is helping clear a library in St Bride's, and he sees a grubby looking man he does not know. On closer insection the stranger is wearing monk's clothing underneath his coat. Neither speaks and suddenly books by the stranger burst into flames.

"How now, father! It must be either you or I that fired those papers!" Stewart exclaims, grabbing hold of the man, who cries, *"Parce mihi, Domini!"* - *"Spare me, Lord"* - in Latin[31].

Stewart later reported to the Parliamentary Committee he was surprised the man spoke Latin; others around him had assumed it was French and had tried to attack him.

Bear in mind the context: shouting anything in Latin during the Fire would have been about as sensible as crying out *"Allah Akbar"* in New York, on 9/11.

Whatever the motivation for this man to cry out in a language that identified him as an 'enemy', it did him no harm. After Stewart handed him over to the authorities he disappeared, like all the other arsonists who were taken into protective custody by James.

Wednesday 5th September
The Fire has seemingly reached its destination and grinds to a halt.

A huge encampment of improvised tents forms in Moorfields, to the north of the City. Thousands compete for limited water and food. Troops are sent in to maintain order.

The King organises food supplies and canvas for tents.

However, the War with the Dutch is going badly, shipping is restricted, supplies are low, many suffer for a lack of decent food. Dogs and cats are killed and eaten; there is desperation.

Charles II also declared the Fire an Act of God: this meant all tenants had to continue to pay rent, as well as find money to rebuild their homes[32]. Landlords were exempt from any duty to them.

Understandably this legal declaration causes widespread dismay, the King's decision seems calculated to wipe the City's slate clean. London was now demoralised, deserted and destroyed.

Carte Blanche

<u>Thursday 6th September</u>

Robert Hooke looks out of his window at the devastation around him.

Uniquely, miraculously, I'd say *unbelievably*, Gresham College, where he lives and teaches Geometry, is untouched by the Fire.

It is one of very few significant City buildings not to have been devastated.

Robert Hooke was pretty much the only man in London who didn't have to move after the Fire. There's a knock at the door, it's the City Fathers, they need a base of operations as their Guildhall headquarters are smoke.

The City Administration moves into Gresham College and everyone except Hooke is forced to move out. Hooke is appointed Surveyor of the City and begins to map out the roads and buildings in the vicinity. It seems he had the necessary equipment to hand.

<u>Tuesday 11th September</u>
Hooke's' friend Christopher Wren, amongst others, produces an elaborate street plan for a new, more majestic London, with long straight roads and monuments.

One includes a plan for a forty foot bronze statue of the Protestant Martyr, Charles I. Before the Fire is completely out, Wren and Hooke already have plans for a new City ready.

Hooke and Wren were the two core members of the Royal Society, and had worked closely together for years. Hooke as Surveyor of the City and Wren as Architect of St Paul's and soon after as King's Surveyor of Works, dominated the rebuilding of London.

Wren's street plan was ready just five days after the Fire died. Hooke's survey of the still smouldering City must have been completed *before that.* With the City administration sharing his college building, decisions were made in record time. Amidst War, Disease, Fire and

Famine, Wren and Hooke worked calmly and efficiently. I find this chilling.

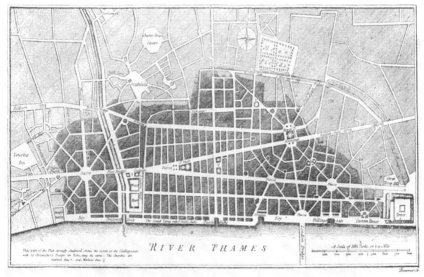

Sir CHRISTOPHER WREN'S PLAN *for* Rebuilding *the* CITY *of* LONDON *after the* Great Fire *in* 1666.

London. Published as the Act directs, by Alex' Hogg, at the Kings Arms N°16, Paternoster Row

Wren's Street Plan for a new London

In Lisa Jardine's biography, *"The Curious Life of Robert Hooke, The Man who Measured London"*, she says *"London's great catastrophe heralded what appears to have been the happiest and most fulfilling period of Hooke's life"*[33].

He was a very strange man, no doubt partly as a result of his father's suicide. He, like his father, was a dyed-in-the-wool Royalist. He was also a first-rate scientist, crafting his own microscope he had become famous for his book, *Micrographia*, which contains dozens of amazing hand drawn pictures of grain and mites.

And then there's his study of the flea.

Hooke made his famous flea drawing in 1665, the year of the Plague. Of course at this time the link between fleas and the plague was not popularly understood. No one in the world had seen anything like it before. Given the context, I find it disturbing.

Hooke worked at the Royal Society as the engineer and equipment maker, responsible for the apparatus needed to conduct experiments. The success of the Society's meetings depended on his skill as an engineer, and he was rarely found wanting. He was a scientist, a daily nutmeg imbiber, and deeply scarred.

Hooke self-medicated with great alacrity each day, essentially using his body as a laboratory. His diary is full of references to what he took – for example, tinctures of lead and mercury - and how it made him feel.

He experimented with combinations of substances. He sought out new ingredients, including the first ship that arrived in London carrying the famed *Bhang* of India, which was some kind of hashish. He was also a friend of Abraham Cowley.

He kept faithful accounts of his physick-taking in his diary, for example,

1 August 1675
Took volatile Spirit of Wormwood which made me very sick... and purged me in the morning. Drank small beer and Sal-amoniack. I purge 5 or 6 times very easily... this is certainly a great Discovery in Physick. I hope that this will dissolve that vicious slime that hath so much tormented me in my stomach and guts. Deus Prosperat[34].

Interestingly his diary also contains this:

30 October 1673
...at Dr Wrens, he very sick with physic taking the day before.

Wren, it seems, loved his physic too, so was not the straight-laced gent we are lead to believe.

These were characters with strongly held and severely tested beliefs. Wren and Hooke were at the centre of the Royal Society and Science, and they were also central in the City's recovery from the Fire. They both had deep-seated reasons, dating from their childhoods, for hating Lions of the City: they were Unicorns.

So, with some trepidation, I include this suggestion: that given War, Fire and Famine had visited London at the Stuarts' behest, perhaps they were trying to enact a God's own style revenge. It would seem to fit their world-view, their desire for retribution, to prevent further insurrections in the future by utterly decimating the population, the City mob.

Plague was considerably better understood than is often realised: doctors would prescribe nutmeg to the rich, and were aware that flea-bites were seen around the swollen, puss-filled blisters that appeared on the skin of the afflicted. This knowledge was all available to Robert Hooke, who obviously took a keen interest in the flea.

Some of the world's best medical minds had spent the centuries since the first outbreaks trying to understand and control this disease. Cleanliness and nutmeg seemed to be the best advice, with some Arab doctors noting long ago that where there were no rats there was no plague.

The Plague that hit London in 1665 was extremely unusual. There was nothing like it in intensity anywhere else in Europe, nor had there been for many years. It came in very quickly, and very quickly the great and the good moved out. The poor were left to die.

The gates of the City were locked shut. You needed a clean bill of health to leave, and these were expensive.

London became a city of death. At least 100,000, maybe as many as 250,00 people died, even as those in the know about nutmeg, and could afford it, walked the streets with impunity... or should that be immunity?

Hooke's study of the flea sticks out to me, it wouldn't have been beyond his skill, had he been asked, to introduce a host of rats and their fleas into London. A single ship carried the plague into the City and a series of terrible decisions made that crisis a disaster.

Someone gave the Lord Mayor *scientific advice* during the Summer of 1665, to kill all the cats and dogs in London. This was done and the rats had proliferated.

Hooke was so hated by the Whigs that Sir Isaac Newton had all his portraits burnt, and many of his achievements and contributions have been down-played.[35] He was quietly removed from history.

There was a profound personal and professional antagonism between Hooke and Newton, ostensibly about who first suggested the inverse square law of gravitation. That honour actually belongs to Hooke, but history awards it to Newton. Their antagonism would have been further compounded by their contrasting beliefs: Newton was very much a Whig, Hooke a Tory.

They both saw the other as *False Brethren.*

Wren and Hooke were right in the eye of the storm. It's hard to say exactly what went on, but I think you get the general idea -

- The Fire was deliberate, all the witnesses thought so; the rebuilding of London would create a new capital, built in stone. This would prove a valuable recruitment and training ground for Masons, and provide possible candidates for the king's Scottish Freemasonry. The City would be made anew, and under Stuart supervision.

- The War was started to drive a wedge between the two Protestant powers, so Charles could keep taking money from his cousin Louis, and eventually use this antagonism to move England back toward the old church.

- The Famine, food shortages caused by the War were predictable, the rise in food prices forced the poorest city dwellers back to the land and their traditional role as subsistence farmers

- The Plague, I suggest, *could* have been nurtured into being by a small group of fanatics around the Crown. A revenge of Biblical proportions for the execution of King Charles I.

The scale of it is a bit overwhelming, there was never really a *Eureka* moment for me, just the more I read around the time, the stranger it seemed.

How were Wren and Hooke so lucky and well prepared?

James II had a notorious hatred for the London rabble, but became the hero of the hour riding round the City?

Dozens of witnesses are several different locations saw him rescue those who had been caught, or accused, of arson.

What happened to John Stewart's prisoner, who had clearly started a fire?

What the hell was John Graunt doing turning off the water to London? He was never punished. This was probably down to the fact he was well-liked by Charles II, who had insisted Graunt be made a member of the Royal Society when it began in 1660.

Graunt's inexplicable intervention was enough to make disaster inevitable. The catastrophe that followed was consistently described, by credible witnesses, as unnatural.

These first-hand accounts are often dismissed out of hand because it disagrees with what we British are taught in Primary School.

As with the teaching of religion, some lessons have to be learnt early, before you become a teenager and start questioning things. I'm not aware of any religion that waits until the child reaches maturity then presents him or her with a balanced argument about the merits of the faith. Indoctrination relies on the credulity of the indoctrinated. It's interesting that every child in Britain learns so early about the Great Fire in particular.

These events are embedded in our national psyche but the way they are taught is not credible on closer examination.

The mental effort to assimilate this information was greater than that when I saw Shakespeare's signatures and realised I had to change my mind. This stuff is deeply embedded within all of us; for many it's the first thing they remember learning at school.

I never expected to come across this information. I know to some it will be deeply unwelcome, and may generate some hostility. For everyone else, I hope, after the shock and rejection, this will help them better understand the country we are from, who governs us, and what they do to maintain control.

Too many people witnessed fires starting far away from the main action. Thomas Middleton was there and was certain. Members of Parliament published a report directly implicating the Duke of York: these were lawyers, bankers and aristocrats – not people to risk their reputations on a conspiracy theory officially published in Parliamentary proceedings.

James Stuart and his retinue rescued people accused of arson, some seemingly using a code-phrase to identify themselves. Holmes and Bloodworth were rewarded by the Stuarts for their respective war-crimes and ineptitude. The Stuarts had punished them publicly, then sometime later, privately promoted them.

Lastly there was the clumsy and tragic fate of Robert Hubert, whose story will lead us back to the inscription on the Monument and how it was official history between 1681 and 1830 that Catholics had started the Fire.

Monumental Failure

Robert Hubert, a French son of a watchmaker, confessed to starting the fire. Few believed him, but he offered himself up as a willing sacrifice to London's anger and suspicion.

It seems the authorities, Lord Mayor Bloodworth included, were reluctant to oblige him. I'm suggesting that by claiming responsibility for the Fire, Hubert may have ruined their preferred narrative about the Dutch.

The authorities didn't want him to confess but he had, so what could they do?

Reading about him and the trial it seems many who were involved were a bit embarrassed.

He could provide some detail to his claim, but essentially everyone including the Judge that sentenced him to death thought he was a fantasist. He was dissolute and depressed, a loner of no fixed abode and with no regular income who seemed to enjoy the attention his confession gave him.

The judge presiding said he hoped Hubert's execution would put an end to all the conspiracy theories surrounding the fire.

And so Robert Hubert died at Tyburn on 27th October 1666, found guilty by a jury that included Thomas Farriner, of starting the Great Fire of London. Farriner, therefore, achieved some sense of closure, Hubert had set fire to his shop, and that explained the intensity of the heat.

In 1681, when the phrase about "Popish frenzy" was added to the Monument, Charles II was still without a legitimate heir and his brother James, a Roman Catholic, would succeed him in 1685. The last years of Charles' reign saw increased antagonism with the City: he even revoked the City's warrant, the legal basis of its power and independence.

James was also deeply unpopular with the merchant class, and he fought for the nation's favour with his bastard nephew, the Duke of Monmouth. James had the legal claim, but Monmouth was charismatic and Protestant.

Amazingly, Monmouth accused James of starting the Fire[36].

This was in the context for a battle for public support, so why would Monmouth make such a claim if he thought no-one would believe it?

Perhaps he was trying to tap into anti-Catholic feeling, but why that specific accusation? History is silent on this as not long after Monmouth was executed.

The Mayor of London in 1681, Sir Patience Ward, was an ardent Protestant and like many he feared what would happen when James became King. These fears were realised in 1685 when James II used the Monmouth Rebellion as a justification for mass executions of his enemies.

The 'Bloody Assizes' as they were known were an attempt to scare people into submission. One Judge Jeffries became especially infamous, organising executions with great alacrity whenever and wherever the opportunity arose. He was married to Sir Thomas Bloodworth's daughter, by arrangement of James II.

James had said he would not compromise. His father had compromised and had been executed: James intended to reign.

James had also, very quickly, created a standing army of about 20,000 men, they were encamped on Hounslow Heath, a day's march from the City. He was the subject of a satire, which nearly everyone in Britain knows: James Stuart was the 'Grand Old Duke of York, who had 10,000 men..."

A standing army was unprecedented in English history; paying soldiers when there was no war to fight was an unnecessary cost. It was considered by many to be the act of a despot, contrary to English liberty, and it certainly didn't help that James appointed and promoted Catholic officers.

In 1681 James's rule was still to come, but in a context where the next in line to the throne was accused by his nephew of setting fire to the nation's capital, Patience Ward had a plaque put up in Pudding Lane, which read...

'Here by ye permission of heaven, hell broke loose upon this protestant city from the malicious hearts of barbarous papists, by hand of their agent Hubert, who confessed, and on ye ruines of this place declared the fact for which he was hanged (vizt) that here began that dredfull fire, which is described and perpetuated on and by the neighbouring pillar. Erected Anno 1681 in the Majoraltie of Sr Patience Ward Kt.'

It was Patience Ward fearing a return to Catholicism under James II who had added the phrase about "*Popish frenzy*" to the Monument. In 1830 someone decided to quietly remove it, it was no longer history and Robert Hubert is now pretty much unknown.

Legal Fiction

When Parliament met, on 18th September, they passed a famous bit of legislation, called *Cestui Qui Vie* – he who lives.

Essentially, people were to be treated as if they were boats on the water and if they failed to appear after seven years, could be declared dead. This incorporation of maritime law into the law of the land meant the

Crown would be able to claim any property from those who had not survived the fire, famine, war and disease.

This Act of Parliament was the first order of business when the Commons sat, and it is worth considering why.

In the wake of some similar national disasters other pieces of controversial legislation have been passed, somehow already drafted, just after a national emergency. Famous examples include the Patriot Act after 9/11, and the Nazi Enabling Act after the Reichstag Fire in 1933.

The Act effectively equated people, the subjects of the nation, with property. Each person was legally identified as a notional ship, a legal fiction, which meant they could be regarded as an asset.

A lot of people assert this mechanism is still in force today. For example, after 1914 the Bank of England no longer backed its currency with gold. Instead, the taxable income of each subject was offered as surety for any loans.

In other words, the Bank borrowed money and promised to pay it back using the revenues derived from these legal fictions; the legal fictions being the people who had had a company set up in their names which is registered when they were issued with their birth certificates.

A lot has been written about this, the timing of the act, being the first law passed by Parliament in the wake of the fire, certainly marks it as of strategic importance.

The use of maritime law as a means of acquiring unclaimed property from dead people is certainly unusual in the extreme; I believe it was unprecedented in England. That this idea was created off the cuff, as an improvised expedient to deal with the problems caused by the Fire, seems unlikely. It is more likely someone had it ready up their sleeve, and the general population were too busy to notice.

During the weeks following the Fire, people had started to rebuild their homes and businesses on their original plots, but this was not easy.

As stated, the King had already ruled that tenants would have to pay their rent whilst also paying for the reconstruction of their homes.

I think this makes Charles II's intention pretty obvious: he wanted to clear the City and start again.

Hooke mapped out the ground, and there was general agreement that London needed to modernise with wider streets and better building standards. And so, the Royal party tried to delay any fixing of buildings to their old plots, but this soon failed.

Following War, Disease and Fire, Famine threatened as London's economic infrastructure collapsed.

Tens of thousands of people were still living in tents on Moorfields to the north of the City. Many moved out to market towns, but others started returning to their old homes. Living in tents or make-shift shacks, they defied expectation and began again, called to their old homes by unseen forces.

This attachment to the land, even in the centre of the city, proved the undoing of Wren's great ambition.

His new street plan had yet to be approved by Parliament, which was still busy with the *Cestui Qui Vie Act*. The king had no legal power to stop rebuilding in the City.

Charles II rode out to witness the patchy, private reconstruction and cried, returning to Whitehall in silence. Perhaps he was mourning the 40ft bronze of his father that would never be.

The whole-sale reordering of London, the lost opportunity that Hawksmoor and others were so bitter about, was never realised. The narrow, crooked streets of the City were blamed for creating narrow crooked citizens.

Wren had hoped to build great straight, proud roads to foster honourable, obedient subjects. Hawksmoor would later use his churches to try and impose order on the City in a more subtle, less expensive, way.

So, slowly, the City emerged phoenix-like from the flames, and London became the undisputed capital of the world: dominating banking, commerce, navigation, colonization, democracy, science and technology. All a coincidence, of course.

Chapter 6
The Phoenix

Since 1666 the City of London has become the dominant financial centre of the world.

The sun never sets on the assets it controls and it has grown in strength since 2008.

It wants to be the managing agent of the future trillionaires.

In Wall Street they call the City the '*financial Guantanamo Bay*': normal rules do not apply.

American and other Banks set up offices in the City so they can do things that would be illegal back home. The City is self-regulated, which is why not a single banker has been prosecuted for decades despite regular corruption scandals. The bankers must be free to trade, the story goes, or they'd would lose confidence in the City and move out. This is true: they'd have to go home and obey the law.

Gross inequality and environmental degradation, invasion, conquest and desolation lie in the City's wake. The City of London is one of the most dangerous and destructive institutions on earth. It gets away with it because it makes the rich richer.

Of course, the City Bankers did not invent this reality; they have merely perfected and honed it, subjugating much of the world in the process. Every Empire is rich, every Empire is strong, how to create and sustain these conditions is the real trick, and this was better understood by the Lions of the City Banks than the Unicorns in the Royal Court.

Charles I was crowned in 1625, but by 1640 his relationship with parliament was so bad he never called another election.

Charles invoked ancient privileges and ignored recent legislation when he illegally asserted his privilege to collect Tonnage and Poundage. Tonnage was a tax on wine, Poundage an import and export tax on all goods. By setting and collecting these Charles hoped to control trade, constrict it if necessary, and impose royal command.

It proved to be his downfall. The forces of international trade were more powerful than the king. His arbitrary actions were disturbing the commerce of the bankers.

In 1642, five renegade members of parliament had evaded Charles by hiding in the City, which had, as previously noted, shut its gates on the king.

Utterly humiliated Charles had no choice but to leave London and start the Civil War by raising his standard in Northampton.

His son Charles II had been through royal hell and back when, restored to the throne in 1660, he took up office in Westminster. The merchants who had arranged Charles I's demise must have been anxious to strike up good relations with his son. I'm sure they offered very generous terms.

Charles II quickly established a cosy relationship with the City's money-men, who were only too happy to indulge the morays of the new king.

Things looked good for the bankers; Charles II was affable, self-indulgent and completely relaxed about the country subsidising his divine rule. He built up debts with five of the largest goldsmiths in the City, equal to billions in today's money.

When, in 1672, Robert Holmes attacked the Dutch Smyrna convoy in the English Channel he had committed a war crime.

But it helped the King, who was always short of cash, and was entitled to most of the booty. The war that followed also gave Charles all the reason he needed to renounce his debts. He told his bankers he could repay the interest on their loans, but not the loan itself, until the war ended.

This bankrupted five major goldsmith businesses and left about ten thousand other wealthy families without their savings. It was known as the *Great Stop*. [37]

This seems to have been a deliberate use of royal power to destroy the bankers who had killed his father. It seems likely that Charles had planned this revenge, as well as the others, while in exile in France. To have killed the bankers as traitors would have been difficult, so Charles became rich by bankrupting and humiliating them.

To the bankers this was a fate worse than death: they were poor. So when, on 5th November 1688, the Bankers helped organise the invasion of William of Orange, it was the City's turn for revenge. The demise of the Stuart Kings signaled the ascendancy of the City over the Nation.

William would act like a king, wear the robes, perform the public functions, but was not the captain of the ship of state: he was the figure-head. He was expected to lead from the front and attract attention while the ship was steered by the navigators of the City.

England and especially London was now more like Venice, an oligarchy, than France, a monarchy.

This arrangement frustrated William, who, as leader of the Dutch, had been used to more control. But he was given what he wanted, support for his life-long war against Louis XIV.

By 1690 he even had the backing of the Pope for the battle of the Boyne in Ireland. Though William was a deeply committed Protestant the Pope favoured him over the recently deposed, and Catholic, James Stuart, the usurped king of England and Scotland, now a servant of Louis XIV of France, for the control of Catholic Ireland.

Politics!

A New Religion

By 1694, William's war with the French was stretching public finances.

Gold was needed to build and provision new war ships for the Royal Navy. So, a Tonnage act was passed, stating anyone who would loan the state £1.2million would have their loan guaranteed at 8% by £140,000 taken annually from the tax on wine.

These Acts of Parliament were common: a deal would be arranged beforehand, then turned into legislation that MPs would approve.

Tonnage arrangements were traditionally reviewed annually: this one lasted for four years, so this was all pretty standard practice.

What was different about this Act is that it allowed for £1.2million to be collected by public subscriptions, the money to be given to a Company, which would use the tonnage money to guarantee them the 8% interest rate.

This public subscription was taken up by King William, who invested £10,000, the maximum allowed for any one share-holder. Many of the great and good did the same for themselves and their children. The £1.2 Million was raised in twelve days. This fund, called in the Act of Parliament a *fondi*, which is an old Italian banking term, was to be incorporated as the *Governor and Bank of England.*

After listing a load of things the Bank couldn't do, for example, buy and sell merchandise, the Act states in section 27, called, *"In what Things they may nevertheless do,[38]"*

"Provided that nothing herein conteined shall any wayes be construed to hinder the said Corporac[i]on from dealeing in Bills of Exchange or in buying or selling Bullion Gold or Silver..."

This gave the Bank the right to issue Bills of Exchange, paper money, it was privately owned but with an inspiring, suitably patriotic name. The 1694 Tonnage Act actually mortgaged the country to create the Navy, and the people of England would be forever in its debt.

The Bank of England's issue of paper money at interest was the industrialisation of a highly profitable business banks had run for years, centuries even, as no one really knew much gold was in their reserves. People had to trust the bankers when they said the coffers were full.

A loss of faith could cause catastrophic panics, riots and revolutions.

So, the Bank of England, with its royal patronage, fancy name and patriotic duty to help build the Navy, was something every true-blue Englishman would support and believe in. It was a new religion, a belief system, based on national pride, profit and war.

With its £1.2 Million in reserves the Bank started to issue £1 and £2 notes, with a value of about £10million.

This was based on the banking practice of fractional reserves, which is still the norm today. The £10million loaned out at 8% would require £800,000 in interest payments in the first year. This interest could not be covered by the paper money: there wasn't enough of it.

So some people had to pay back some or all of their debt in gold or silver. The Bank of England turned symbols and signs on pieces of paper into gold. In a year they nearly doubled their *fondi*.

Greedy God

The eternal demand for interest to be paid was at the heart of Empire.

You had to bring back more than you'd started with, or your offering to the high altar of Capitalism would be rejected and you were cast out of heaven.

The Bank literally made a fortune every year by incentivising aggressive Imperial expansion. The way the Bank was set up necessitated the constant acquisition of new lands and goods. This engine of Empire was founded on the back of an Act of Parliament ostensibly about a tax on wine.

It was ostensibly about a tax on tea that caused the American War for Independence. But it was really about banking, as *Irish Freemason, Benjamin Franklin,* said,

"The colonies would gladly have borne the little tax on tea and other matters, had it not been that England took away from the colonies their money, which created great unemployment and dissatisfaction. Within a year, the poor houses were filled. The hungry and homeless walked the streets everywhere. The inability of the colonists to get power to issue their own money permanently out of the hands of George III and the International Bankers was probably the Prime reason for the Revolutionary War"[40].

Why was that so important, Ben?

"That is simple. In the Colonies we issue our own money. It is called Colonial Scrip. We issue it in proper proportion to the demands of trade and industry to make the products pass easily from the producers to the consumers. In this manner, creating for ourselves our own paper money, we control its purchasing power, and we have no interest to pay no one".
(41)

Franklin and the other Revolutionaries knew that buying paper money at interest from the Bank of England was a subtle form of subjugation, a form of financial serfdom, a slavery made of mind-forged manacles.

St George and the Dragon, St George's Wapping

It was this American desire to make their own money for free that drove them to War. Otherwise they would forever be paying more than a pound for a pound, and their wealth drawn out of America by the Bank.

Unfortunately, since 1913, the Federal Reserve Bank has done to America what the Bank of England had tried to do. Both institutions deftly blur the boundaries between public and private and leave the layman ill-informed about what is really going on.

Miserly Company

The City's Colonisation of North America began under the control of the Virginia Company, which had been incorporated in 1606. The Virginia Company charter had given them permission to establish settlements on the East coast between then 34th and 41st parallels of latitude.

This company organised and paid for the first set of colonists, who created James Town. The *Pilgrim Fathers,* as they are otherwise known, were there on Virginia Company business, as every colonist was expected to work to create financial returns for the shareholders.

Later came the Massachusetts Bay Company, incorporated in 1629, which occupied much of New England, and the Hudson Bay Company, which was the world's largest landowner, controlling about 15% of North America.

All three companies suffered catastrophic losses during the War of Independence. Shareholder value was replaced by a declaration of rights and some lost a fortune.

Gradually, the joint stock Companies listed in London spread out across the world and were the building blocks of the City's financial Empire.

In 1616 the Somers Isle Company was incorporated to facilitate state-backed piracy. The colony in Bermuda was used to launch privateering raids against the Spanish Gold fleets. For *some reason* we were nearly always at war with the Spanish, so this highly profitable piracy was legal.

The Monarch received the largest single share of every ship taken.

Sir Francis Drake, known as *El-Draco* – The Dragon – in Spanish, used to advise his pirates not to fill their pockets too full of coins, as the weight might drag them down and drown them. It seems the *El-Draco* was a prudent corporate pirate.

In 1618 the Guinea Company was incorporated to facilitate the sale and transportation of human beings from Africa, whom the City had decided did not have souls, so were no better than cattle.

This ability to treat other people as alien or other has tremendous economic advantages. Slaves were commodities, treated like animals, put in chains and forced to cultivate sugar, tobacco and cotton in the American colonies.

In 1672, the Royal African Company was incorporated, originally known as the Company of Royal Adventurers Trading to Africa.

By its charter issued in 1660 it was granted a monopoly over English trade along the West coast of Africa, with the principle objective being the search for gold.

In 1663 a new charter was obtained which also mentioned the trade in slaves. The Company was owned by James II and it replaced the Guinea Company which, it was felt, was making far too much money to not be controlled by the Crown.

Then there was India, a culture of immemorial provenance and mellifluous diversity. Not that that mattered. What mattered to Queen Elizabeth I when she incorporated the East India Company in 1600 was the sub-continent's incredible wealth.

She gave the City Bankers God's permission to use Imperial steel in the acquisition of Indian gold.

What gave them all hope were the technological advances in the art of war. She was aware the Indians were less proficient at modern military machinery in general, and naval combat in particular.

It obviously escaped her notice that Indians had a sense of contentment and decency that meant sailing halfway round the world to rob and kill people may not have entered their minds in the first place.

India was incredibly rich, accounting for about 25% of the world economy. At the same time England's counted for about 3%.

Indian spices were part of the trade, but, more important were the manufactured goods, textiles especially but also jewellery and furniture.

At the time, the ruler of most of modern India, the Mughal Emperor Akbar the Great, was worth more than all the Kings and Queens of Europe combined.

Gold from Europe had gone to India since before the Roman Empire, with textiles and spices flowing back. Roman Senators complained about this trade imbalance, and even before that, Alexander the Great had tried to conquer India for this reason.

Its wealth was legendary and this 5,000 year-old cultural trade-imbalance was about to meet the might of mechanised monetarism.

Recently, Utsa Patnaik an economist, published a study with the Columbia University Press. The report calculated that over two hundred years the East India Company and then the Empire extracted about $45 Trillion of wealth from India.[41]

When the Empire left, India had been crippled, accounting for less than 5% of the world economy. 90% of the people lived in poverty and literacy levels had dropped to less than 20%.

This deliberate debasement of indigenous culture was Imperial policy; you had to keep the buggers down, or they'd take back what you'd stolen from them.

Inglorious Empire, the book by the Indian Statesman Shashi Tharoor, is a forensic and erudite analysis of the English East India Company's behaviour in India, and contains dozens of examples of its practices.

We've got time for only two.

Textiles were a staple of the Indian economy; they were masters of the craft, producing fabrics so fine you could pull a Sari through a wedding ring.   The Company wanted to sell English factory-made cotton to the world, and saw the Indian textile economy as a threat.

So, they taxed the export of Indian cloth, destroyed the hand-looms on which they were made, and at least once cut off the thumbs of the weavers. For English cloth to conquer, Indian cloth had to suffer.

The inferior English cotton, grown on the slave plantations of southern United States, manufactured by the factory workers of England, replaced the indigenous craft tradition.

As part of his resistance of the Empire, Gandhi encouraged Indians to make their own cotton. He called it *home-spun*, an act of passive, defiant independence. That's why there is a spinning-wheel on the flag of India.

The Railway network in India is often cited as one of the great benefits of Imperial rule.

In reality the trains were built using Indian taxes and labour for the benefit of the Empire. Fares for passengers were high, and subsidised the very low rates business paid for freight.

In the 19th Century it cost about $2,000 to build a mile of track in America. In India it cost $18,000. You can bet your bottom dollar that $16,000 price difference didn't go to the workers. Everything the Empire did in India was for profit. They trained the local soldiers to bayonet people if at all possible as bullets are expensive.

Tharoor describes four guiding principles that the Company operated by:

One: No Charity.

Helping the poor native wasn't just frowned upon, it could get you arrested and deported. This strict ban on empathy for the conquered is very interesting psychologically, it encourages the sense of otherness that is the precondition to cruelty and exploitation.

Studies show the kinder you are to someone the more you'll come to like them. There's also the opposite: randomly punch someone and within five minutes you'll have thought of a dozen reasons why they deserved it.

As a company, as a government, as individuals there was to be no quarter given, no kindness, everything was done by the book, often with unnecessarily tragic consequences.

Two: Free Market.

Everything was for sale in India: even if people were starving and someone else could pay more for their food, the highest bidder won. This mechanism caused several famines, most recently in Bengal in 1943 where about three million people starved.

Winston Churchill was buying up wheat for stockpiles in Europe, he was told by local officials that food was scarce, but he ignored them.

Later, with characteristic humanity and humility he said, "*I hate Indians. They are a beastly people with a beastly religion. The famine was their own fault for breeding like rabbits.*" He also inquired if Gandhi was "*dead yet*". This is just one example, but it shows how much the more the market meant than the Indian people, who were treated like a commodity.

Three: Malthusianism.

Thomas Malthus was an economist working for the Company.

His thinking became gospel within the Empire, every *Company Man* would learn about him.

He said there was only so much to go round, only so much gold, only so much steel, only so much food that could be grown. So, if a particular area had stability for too long, people living in peace and prosperity would eventually have too many children for that area to bear. Too much peace was bad for business: death and destruction were economically desirable.

Overpopulation was a problem like the over-supply of any other resource, if there was too much of it, it would have an impact on profitability and that had to be dealt with.

This is why the Empire let people starve, fundamentally they were superfluous to requirements, and therefore a liability. Some allege this is also why the Empire encouraged factional fighting between Muslims and Hindus.

Malthus reckoned the Earth could only sustain one Billion people, some people advocate for that number today.

Four: Budget for profit.

This is the easiest to describe: all of the above add up to the bottom line. It was all done for money.[42]

This four-part model was the rule across the Empire, there were no sentimental exceptions. It was genocide for profit.

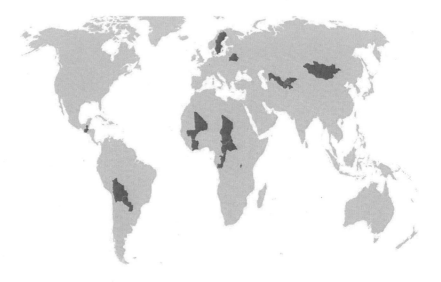

Map of the World showing countries that Britain
Has **NOT** attacked

By the time the British reached China greed had taken over to an extent that is hard to believe.

Again, as a Briton, I had to find this out for myself, from friends with Chinese backgrounds, or just from reading around. We are never taught this, it is kept from us because it shows our country in a bad light, our rulers want us to continue to sleep-walk through our history.

Britain fought two 'Opium Wars', (1839-42, and then, 1856-1860), with China, these wars were waged because the Qing rulers of China didn't want Britain to flood their country with that highly addictive drug.

Britain bombed the Chinese into submission twice, and as a result millions became addicted. Britain also demanded compensation, essentially they wanted the Chinese to pay for the bombs that had been dropped on them. Hong Kong was given over to the British for ninety-nine years as compensation for the interruption of free trade.

Many great fortunes were made in the 'China Trade', in the U.S. the Astor family, the Forbeses, the Russells and the Delanos became some of America's first millionaires through this trade. In Britain, the Sassoon family set up their private bank with their opium profits.

This is the Malthusian approach to business, as practised by the British, we would kill people in order to make others drug addicts, and this was the 'right' thing to do economically. Other races of people were not afforded the dignity of being treated humanely.

Businesses were encouraged to exploit 'lesser races', this wasn't just racism as such, it was a colder kind of calculation that played on fear and a sense of otherness to gain power.

It is with us now and it has a pedigree.

Nearly all of the expertise that helped set up the Companies, the legal and financial institutions that built the Empire, and the stories that would sustain it, came from Venice, of which more soon.

Malthus's 'philosophy' and the deeply flawed interpretation of the theory of evolution now labelled 'Neo-Darwinism' lurk behind the current trend among the rich and powerful. The 1%.

They have concluded – *"scientifically and dispassionately"* - that there are *too many people on earth*, they say, so compassion is misplaced sentimentality in the face of Darwinian nature.

111

This despite the fact we could sustainably feed, cloth and house about 10billion people, using today's technology.

This would obviously not be easy, but is not impossible.

The fact this would require the 1% to share what they have is obviously unacceptable to them, why should the *superior* help the *inferior*? This Malthusian/Darwinian 'logic' has been used to justify all kinds of horrors.

Through Darwinism and Malthusianism the ideology of Empire has gained a tighter grip on debate, and the Tory vision of *us and them*, of the *worthy* and the *great unwashed*, is becoming increasingly normalised and entrenched, but a better world is possible.

An Old Hope

"There are two ways of viewing the Government's duty in matters affecting economic and social life. The first sees to it that a favoured few are helped and hopes that some of their prosperity will leak through, sift through, to labour, to the farmer, to the small business man. That theory belongs to the party of Toryism, and I had hoped that most of the Tories left this country in 1776".[43]
Franklin Delano Roosevelt, 1932, Speech accepting Democrat Party Candidacy for President.

"I am firmly of the belief that if we are to arrive at a stable peace it must involve the development of poorer countries... It can't be done by eighteenth-century methods". Said Roosevelt to Churchill.

"Who's talking eighteenth-century methods?" Churchill enquired.

"Which ever of your ministers recommends a policy which takes wealth in raw materials out of a colonial country, but which returns nothing to the people of that country...

Twentieth century methods involve bringing industry to these colonies. Twentieth century methods include increasing the wealth of a people by increasing their standard of living, by educating them, by bringing them sanitation – by making sure they get a return for the raw wealth of their community".

"Mr President", Churchill cried, *"I believe you are trying to do away with the British Empire. Every idea you entertain about the structure of the post-war world demonstrates it".*[44]

Taken from *"As He Saw It"*, by Elliot Roosevelt, assistant to his father.

Why is a 20th century American President being cited in a book supposedly about 18th century Churches? Because the power structures that Hawksmoor's work celebrated, the Empire, was still in effect then, is still in effect today, and what Franklin Delano Roosevelt did shows that it is possible to things differently, better. . .

Roosevelt inherited a fortune, his Delano family wealth came from opium, but he was motivated by something other than greed, he had a creed.

He was a Freemason, famously putting the eye on the pyramid onto the dollar bill.

However, it seems clear he was not a Scottish Freemason, with its associations with Tory hierarchy. He must, it seems to me, have been part of the Irish tradition, identifying with its more egalitarian and spiritual values.

Roosevelt was no angel, he forced Japanese Americans into internment camps during World War two, and is a *bete noire* of the libertarian neo-liberals of today. What he did economically, however, offers a vision of how a different, kinder world is possible.

Throughout the 1930s he invested in projects that would lift ordinary people out of poverty, great dams to provide clean electricity, social security and in work benefits. He even created an American national health service, which was quickly and quietly dismantled after his death.

Had he lived, the structures he created: the United Nations, the International Monetary Fund and World Bank, were going to spread this approach across the world. By investing in infrastructure and education Roosevelt intended to encourage an educated peace and stability.

The IMF and World Bank now operate on what I'm calling the Imperial model now, forcing loans and the sale of national assets onto poorer nations. This is exactly the type of exploitation they were created to defeat, they were, for a while, genuinely interested in human development.

Roosevelt crafted International Banking protocols, which were negotiated at the Bretton Woods conference in 1944. Had they still been in place, they would have made the 2008 financial crisis impossible.

Money, in Roosevelt's view, was the servant not the master. He had banned bankers and their representatives from Bretton Woods, where the world's financial architecture was being designed. He kicked them out of the temple.

Bankers banned from a conference about regulating banks. The opposite of the neo-liberal, laissez-faire approach that predominates now. He was re-elected four times, is one of the greatest figures of the 20th Century, but gets very little press nowadays. It obvious why: he set a dangerously egalitarian precedent.

Following the Great Depression of 1929 bankers had very little credit with the public.

Their response to Roosevelt's election was to try and organise a coup, led by the American War Hero, Major General Smedley Butler.[45]

Happily, Butler was more loyal to his country than to the people who thought they owned it.

Butler's Book, *War is a Racket*, is a fascinating insight into what was going wrong with American foreign policy. He said as a Marine he'd been a dupe and a hit-man for Empire, killing for corporations. This was the 1930's. Smedley Butler was a hero, but it seems very little has changed. Perhaps they've come full-circle.

Roosevelt said, *"The money changers have fled from their high seats in the temple of our civilization. We may now restore that temple to the ancient truths. The measure of the restoration lies in the extent to which we apply social values more noble than mere monetary profit".*[46]

It was not Churchill who won the War: it was Roosevelt. Churchill's part is over-emphasized and Roosevelt's down-played, some say his death at the end of the war was an assassination, to prevent his post-war policies being enacted.

He and Churchill didn't get on. Roosevelt's argument was, "I can't believe that we can fight a war against fascist slavery, and at the same *time not work to free people all over the world from a backward colonial policy".*

Churchill replied, *"There can be no tampering with the Empire's economic agreements...They're the foundation of our greatness"*[47].

Churchill was no freedom fighter, and no friend to the common people, he was interested in preserving the Empire and its exploitation of *lesser* races. It was, after all, the way the world worked, as *'Darwin had proved'*.

Roosevelt, had he lived, would have brought about changes to the world economy that would have ended the Empire.

Some years later, President Kennedy brought back some of Roosevelt's policies, which, for the sake of context I should mention were inspired by what Lincoln had done a century before.

For example, Kennedy wanted to give Kwame Nkrumah's government in Ghana nuclear power. This, a few years after Ghana achieved independence from the Empire. The economic effects of this would have been huge, Ghanaians would have had the power to improve their lives – which in the West means watch T.V... maybe they'd have done something else?

The contrast is pretty clear, keeping the buggers down through control of the economy, for the sake of the Imperial Master Race, or build people up, treat them as equals and invest in a shared, constantly improving future.

Today the world's biggest ever infrastructure project, called the 'one belt, one road' initiative is being rolled out across the planet[48].

Bridges, tunnels, ports, railway net-works all being built to help connect the world together economically. It is unlikely you've heard of this, as the rulers of the Anglo-sphere don't want you to know about it.

China is leading this mutual development drive. It is not some act of charity on their part, they need people to be able to buy all the goods they are producing. This $8 trillion investment is quietly ignored by our media, and is under attack from Anglo-Imperial interests because it will tend to undermine their control of resources.

The Imperial model has won out in America, it was already there, but it was driven into the heart of Washington by Churchill after WWII, with the cold-war against Communist Russia. Roosevelt had promised Stalin financial aid after the war, Churchill lobbied the Americans to take a more aggressive stance.

The billions Stalin had been promised never materialised, and given the level of sacrifice Russia made, he was justifiably aggrieved. The Allies betrayed Russia after the end of World War Two and created the 'Cold-War' pretty much out of thin air, conjuring a bogey man out of an ally. Churchill's 'Iron Curtain' speech effectively created the Iron Curtain, a reason for continued militarism: fighting the evils of communism.

The Anglophile establishment in the United States started playing Empire more and more, with encouragement and advice from the British, to pursue their *'shared values'*. The second half of the 20th Century was blighted by an unnecessary and counter-productive geopolitical game, played to keep the other side down, rather than build us all up.

Today's iterations are more personalised and focused through the media we consume.

"Fake News" and "Conspiracy Theories" are both current in our society because those who create state propaganda: the BBC, Fox Network, MSNBC, CNN and so on, do more to put us down than lift us up.

Propaganda is as old as the hills, the state has always tried to define what is and is not acceptable. The Roman Catholic Church spat its dummy in the face of the printing press as it meant they no longer had a monopoly on propaganda, some called the printing press satanic.

The modern parallels are there for the taking.

The Reformation of the Church, made possible by the printing press, caused the powers that be to create a Counter-Reformation, to retrench their power, and so it goes today.

St Mary Woolbnoth's

The Forces of Conservatism work to maintain the status quo, they dehumanise those that threaten their hegemony, the Oligarchs have a shared interest in keeping us down.

They are family

One great example of the Oligarchic nature of British Capitalism is evident in the life and career of the Governor of the Bank of England during the period 1920-44, Montagu Norman.

He was from the same family as William Montagu who had help set up the Order of the Garter in the 14th century, and Charles Montagu, who had set up the Bank of England in the 17th century.

Montagu Norman had worked widely in merchant banking, he had excellent family connections, but his Governorship was controversial because of his support for the Nazis. After the invasion of Czechoslovakia in 1938, Montagu arranged for Czech gold, held in the Bank's of England's vaults, to be made available to the Nazis.[49]

He was under no obligation to be so helpful.

He was, besides, best friends with Hjalmar Schacht, Hitler's minister of economics and Reichsbank president. He was God-father to one of Schact's grandchildren, who had been named *Norman* in his honour.

He later told a Morgan banker, *"Hitler and Schacht are the bulwarks of civilisation in Germany"*. It is tempting here to entertain the theory that the Governor of the Bank of England was funding the Nazis for profit, and this is what some allege.

The kindest interpretation is that Norman was an *'appeaser'* who believed a strong Germany was the best defence against Communist Russia. The policy of appeasement was in truth tacit support for the Nazis in the hope that they and the Russians would destroy each other in a war in Central Europe.

The Governor of the Bank of England during World War Two, meanwhile kept up his extensive connections with Banks that were backing the Nazis.

He had worked for Brown Brothers, which later merged to become Brown Brothers Harriman in 1931. It was while working for this bank that Prescott Bush, father and grandfather of the Bush Presidents, had been caught organising the finances of the Nazis.

One of Hitler's early supporters was Fritz Thyssen, an industrialist, whose finances in America were run by the Union Banking Corporation. Montagu Norman's former employers at Brown Brothers Harriman helped Thyssen manage his money and financed the Nazi "economic miracle" of the 30's.

In 1942 Roosevelt's government prosecuted them all for Trading with The Enemy.[50]

They were far *too posh to punish*, but it had been this same nexus of people who had tried to encourage Smedley Butler to become an American version of Hitler.

Montagu Norman's friends and business associations make his sympathies pretty obvious. He and his fellow travellers in the City were squeezed by Roosevelt's economics, they all breathed a sigh of relief when he died.

But the Empire was still at risk: democratic movements, like Gandhi's in India, began to assert their independence.

The City saw a rapid decline in business, as people all over the world rightly saw the *Roosevelt Model* as preferable, and took loans from Institutions set up to further development.

The infiltration of the World Bank and IMF by friends of Empire took time, now these bodies are rightly despised by people serious about human development. To be clear when the World Bank and IMF were set up is was to *provide an alternative* to exploitative imperial capitalism, not to perpetuate it. Their moral demise has resulted in poverty and deprivation where there could have been prosperity and development.

One of the principle controls Roosevelt imposed on finance was on international currency speculation.

Money could be moved from one country to another, but only for long-term investment, not for short-term profit.

This, along with the gold standard, offered price stability and prevented the kind of profiteering that had caused the Great Depression. This was good for everyone except the Bankers, it brought about the sustained growth in the West enjoyed by the post-war generation.

The Baby-Boomers were beneficiaries of Roosevelt's policies.

Find the Lady

Enter Sigmund Warburg, from an American Banking family, who was based in London.

In 1963 he suggested to the Bank of England that bonds made in another country, that paid interest in a third, were not under their regulatory control. This would mean deals done in the City, but located off-shore, could be exempt from international regulation by the Bank. They would call it the Eurobond market, it was a hustle, a ruse, but potentially incredibly lucrative.[51]

The Governor winked and the rest is history.

In 1963 the *Eurobond* market was worth $50 million, by 1964 over $500Million. In 1980 the Eurobond market was worth $500 billion, by 1988 $4.8 trillion, and in 1997 over 90% of international loans were made on this market. London ruled once more.

Bankers loved it because they could move their client's money wherever they liked, avoiding taxes and restrictions.

By under cutting the Bretton Woods financial agreements the City started to wield serious power again.

In 1964, 11 US banks had branches in the City of London by 1975, fifty eight did. They did business in London that was illegal to do in the US, and so began the systematic siphoning off of wealth that has led us up to today.

City firms operate in Crown territories that allow Trusts to be set up. The Trusts are deliberately difficult to regulate, and are essentially anonymous, leaving the beneficiaries to do as they please.

The Trusts are used by drug cartels and corporations for the same reason, they avoid tax.

Thirteen of the top twenty tax havens owe their allegiance to the British Crown.

Anything up to $50 trillion Dollars is held off shore world-wide, City firms control about half of that. Again, it is hard to say exactly who is benefitting, but obviously, it is the super-rich, the 1%.

Treasure Islands

The United Kingdom maintains a series of financial redoubts and island bases for the Navy, including Gibraltar, Cyprus, Bahrain, Singapore, Hong Kong, Diego Garcia, The Falklands, Bermuda, and islands in the Caribbean as well as, Jersey, Guernsey and the Isle of Man.

The Cayman Islands alone houses 80,000 shell companies, three quarters of all global hedge-funds, about $2 trillion in assets, and is the fifth largest financial centre in the world.

It has a population of about 60,000; most work to service the needs of the Banking sector. Nicholas Shaxton's book, *Treasure Islands*, gives a brilliant overview of the situation.

It was, perhaps, the most obviously bare-faced hypocritical and disingenuous thing I've seen a politician do, when, in 2016, the British Prime Minister, David Cameron (PM 2010-2016), organised an international conference to clamp down on secretive banking laws.

To clamp down on those *banking* laws, but not the regulation of Trust funds, would have been a masterful piece of deception. It failed because it was such a transparently self-serving move: regulate the secretive banks in Switzerland, but let the City trust fund managers go free.

Had his initiative been successful, Cameron would have created more work for the City, as people closed down their bank accounts, they would have needed to use trust funds, or pay tax.

It was the determination of the European Union to clamp down on off-shore tax banking and trust funds, that has led to Brexit. We are led by an oligarchy who only care about their money. [52]

The consequences of this off-shore oligarchy is devastating, and its reach is global.

For example, in 2008, the debt of African countries was $177 billion, between 1970 and 2008 over $944 billion had been siphoned out of the continent into off-shore financial instruments.

The Organised Crime expert, Roberto Saviano, whose book *Gomorrah* earned him a death sentence from the Mafia, is clear where this corruption, that prevents development and peace in the world, comes from.

"If I asked what is the most corrupt place on Earth, you might say it's Afghanistan, maybe Greece, Nigeria, the south of Italy. I would say it is the UK.

It's not UK bureaucracy, police, or politics, but what is corrupt is the financial capital. Ninety per cent of the owners of capital in London have their headquarters offshore... Jersey and the Caymans are the access gates to criminal capital in Europe and the UK is the country that allows it." [53]

The illusion of legitimacy is currently maintained by a nonagenarian lady, with a million pounds hat. The elevation of the British Royal Family in the American Media has been one of the most depressing things I've ever seen on TV.

Thinking about what it means for back-stage politics makes me thoroughly convinced the Empire is winning over the Republic, to the detriment of everyone's interests, except the elite.

Medieval Kingdom

In America, they have theme parks you can go see people wear silly costumes, chat a load of saccharine rubbish, and live in fancy fantasy castles. You have to choose to go and buy a ticket.

In Britain, we have Knights, Lords, Barons, Viscounts, Earls, Dukes Princes and Kings. We also have, Knights of the Garter, Knights of the Bath, Knights of the Thistle, Commanders and Members of the Empire, and this 0.6% of the population owns 69% of the land.

We also have to subsidise this through our taxes.

The culture of deference to the entitled makes England attractive to others who want the same treatment and can pay for it. Billionaires are encouraged to live here on the basis the British will not revolt, we've been trained, over centuries, into passive obedience.

I have heard stories that Billionaires are shown videos of strikes in France, which can get pretty lively, then these are compared with Royal celebrations in the U.K. All those people in Union Jack suits enthusiastically waving their little plastic flags actually attract billionaires to come and live here: Lose – Lose as far as I'm concerned.

The Queen and Monarchy are the tip of the ice-berg in this hereditary hierarchy, of enslavement by birth. The royal family are the living embodiments of inequality, superiority and privilege.

This country is living in the dark ages, and wants to keep the rest of the world there too. We are nearly always one of the principle combatants in international wars, the only products we make of any value are weapons.

Our financial services have taken over from where our Empire left, and the City is the hub of international corruption. Trillions are traded and taxes evaded. Meanwhile the boroughs adjoining the City are some of the poorest parts of Europe.

Hawksmoor planned for all this.

I think his Churches are fascinating, but I think the Tory God they celebrate needs to put everyone out of his misery and move on, change, develop, reincarnate. This story needs a dramatic twist or it will end in tragedy for everyone.

Hawkmoor's Churches form links in a chain in history that go back millennia.

This is not best understood as a conspiracy, it's a continuity which is, every so often, interrupted. These continuities are extremely instructive, they define the effective use of power, these are the forms of politics that have dominated, however despicable they were and remain.

So, to complete this journey, we're now about to visit, a place responsible for much of the unnecessary death and destruction of the middle-ages, which was, non-coincidentally, the precursor to the current Anglo-Empire.

They too created a great City and Empire, but that greatness was bought at an impossible price. Venice is rightly associated with great beauty, terrible cruelty and imminent destruction.

St Mary Woolnoth, City of London

Chapter 7
Serene Republic

As well as being of interest in its own right, the history of Venice, as a model for London, helps broaden the perspective of this book across time and space. This is both fun and necessary. Hawksmoor's vision was writ on an unambiguously ambitious scale: he meant his churches to last a thousand years. They were designed to encapsulate the energy needed to propel the Empire onward, and they succeeded.

Venice was incredibly influential in the creation of the City's designs for Empire. The roots of this go back a long way, some people have described it as a metastasis, like a cancer, this system infected London slowly and surely, creating a City and Empire in its own image.

If you want to understand the City of London, as the embodiment of modern Capitalist Empire, you need to know about this relationship with Venice. The Banking, the Navy, the racism, bigotry and enslavement that became familiar in London found their inspiration in the Serene Republic.

Critics of the City point to Venice as the parent, the role-model and mid-wife of the British Empire, and those critics included some very famous Tories. [54]

Benjamin Disraeli, the Tory Prime Minister who persuaded Queen Victoria to become Empress of India, and take control of the colony from the Company, wrote a couple of books. Disraeli's Premiership marked the end of what some call the '*Whig Century*', the period after the Glorious Revolution that had seen the Whigs in the ascendancy for generations.

In his novel '*Conningsby*', published in 1844, he wrote, *"The great object of Whig leaders in England from the first movement under Hampden to the last most successful one in 1688, was to establish in*

*England a high aristocratic republic on the model of the Venetian....
William the Third told ... Whig leaders, `I will not be a doge.'... They
brought in a new family on their own terms. George I was a doge; George
II was a doge.... George III tried not to be a doge.... He might try to get rid
of the Whig Magnificoes, but he could not rid himself of the Venetian
constitution."* [55]

Disraeli described the Whigs as the '*Venetian*' party and no doubt saw
them as *False Brethren*.

His assertion of the Crown over the Company in India cost its share-
holders a fortune. But that was O.K., because the share-holders were
Whigs, and very few of Disraeli's Tory friends held shares in the East
India Company anymore.

Maybe they sold their shares just in time?

In a shake-up on this scale - who was going to Govern (siphon off the
wealth from) India – there was an opportunity to make a fortune.

The Coronation of George I, in 1714, had been orchestrated by the
Whigs because they wanted a Doge, not a king. According to Disraeli,
William III was invited over in 1688 but wanted to flex his kingly
muscles too much for the bankers' liking, and they did not miss him
when he died.

Red-Coats

The Venetian influence on England goes back a long way further than
this.

In the 1640's, Oliver Cromwell decided that English soldiers should
wear a uniform dyed using Venetian Red, the origin of the British
Army's Red-Coat. This established a new and lucrative trade.

Cromwell was also related by marriage to a Sir Horatio Pallavicini, a
Genoese banker with Venetian connections. He had links to Whig
merchants in the City including John Hampden and Oliver St John, who
had taken King Charles I to court over his illegal imposition of

Poundage on Shipping. Cromwell was part of a complex of families that had *Venetian* sympathies, and it was they who organised and executed the Civil War. (56)

Oliver's ancestor, Thomas Cromwell, had helped Henry VIII dissolve the monasteries, and his family had become rich taking over former Church land.

Thomas Cromwell was one of many English statesmen who had studied at Padua University, the institution created to educate the Venetian nobility in Statecraft. Other famous English graduates of Padua included Francis Walsingham, Robert Bertie, and Henry Wotton: spies and diplomats. Padua taught a humanist curriculum, devoid of the pieties and superstitions of the Roman tradition. The Venetians had a deeply held distaste for the pretensions of Rome to any kind of moral superiority.

Venice had supported Henry VIII's struggle for independence in matters religious. The opportunity to undermine Catholic hypocrisy was too good to miss. There was a deep antagonism between the home of the faith and the centre of trade.

Venice funded many of the printing presses that Martin Luther had used to promote the reformation. Venice played a strategic role in the Protestant revolutions that followed. Also, as maritime powers, England and Venice shared obvious common interests.

Blue Thongs

The link between England and Venice goes back even further, to the official creation of the most exclusive chivalric order in the world.

When Edward III was crowned in 1327, he believed absolutely in his privilege, his destiny and divinity. He set up the Order of the Garter, comprising of the King and twelve companion knights, plus the Prince of Wales and another twelve for him.

These twenty-six people share in a rite that is presided over by the Dean of St George's Chapel, Windsor, who, at a later date, was Sir Christopher

Wren's father. It was set up by Edward to help conquer, or at least pillage, France, after he had deliberately caused an international banking crisis.

The official story is that Edward III started the Order after the Countess of Salisbury, Joan of Kent, had dropped her garter while dancing. The King had picked it up and said, "Shame on him who thinks ill of it". This became the Order's motto and I trust you are as sceptical of this as I am.

Edward III exploited the close relationship he enjoyed with the bankers in the City, and with one bank in particular. The Bardi bank, ultimately based in Florence, was the biggest in the world at the time. It was, therefore, Venice's main competitor.

So, when Edward first asked the Bardi bank for money they said *no problem*, just give us all the wool in England if you fail to make your repayments.

But then he asked for more, and the Bardi bank said *no problem,* just give us all the sheep in England if you fail to keep up with your responsibilities. Edward pushed his credit to breaking point then simply stopped paying, causing the Bardi bank to eventually collapse.

This was an unprecedented move by a European monarch at that time, where did he think he'd get his money from?!? He was clearly a barbarian and a fool. His default undermined Florence's, and Europe's, economy for decades.

Happily for Edward III, he had arranged other sources of money.

He claimed he was the rightful King of France and invaded and pillaged the country, starting what is now called the Hundred Years War. It was this claim that the Order of the Garter was set up to support, and all the Order's membership became supremely rich as a result of their conquests.

In 1344, Edward III's refusal to pay his debts to the Bardi bank of Florence nearly destroyed the wealth of that City.

Bardi's had been the biggest bank in Europe, Florence was Venice's main strategic threat. So, it can't just be a coincidence that, four years before all this, in 1340, Edward had sent an embassy to the Venetian Doge, Gradenigo, announcing his intention to wage war on France, and offering an Anglo-Venetian alliance?

Gradenigo accepted Edward III's offer that all Venetians on English soil would receive all the same privileges enjoyed by Englishmen.

In other words, low tax trade.

In return for this, Gradenigo helped finance Edward III's Hundred Years War - the pillage of France - which had been threatening Venice on land; after the King had bankrupted Venice's main banking rival. (57) These were the sorts of hostile takeovers the Plantagenets specialised in.

The link between Venice and this most famous Order goes back to even before its official creation by Edward III.

The Order has origins going back to the crusades, to Richard I, the 'Lion Heart'.

The following extract is taken from 'A Life of Edward III', by a man called Winstanley.

About the 19 yere of this kinge, he made a solempne feest at Wyndesore, and a greate justes and turnament, where he devysed, and perfyted substanegally, the order of the knyghtes of the garter; howe be it some afferme that this order began fyrst by kynge Rycharde, Cure de Lyon, at the sege of the cytye of Acres; where, in his great necessyte, there were but 26 knyghtes that fyrmely and surely abode by the kynge; where he caused all them to were thonges of blew leyther about theyr legges. And afterwarde they were called the knyghtes of the blew thonge.[58]

So, for some reason, twenty-five knights stayed and helped Richard as he attacked the port city of Acre on the third crusade.

Richard decided this was a good time to tie a blue leather thong to their thighs. Nothing weird about that! All perfectly normal, please move along.

In 1189, after the siege of Acre on the East Mediterranean coast, Richard I had taken the City and given it over to the Venetians.

This was a bit like robbing the Bank of England then giving all the spoils to the guy that drove the van. The Venetians had helped transport the troops and supplies needed for the Crusade to succeed. They now had control of a port on the Levant, and could expect to make duty-free trade with Asia. This seems very, very generous of Richard, a man not known for sharing.

So, the siege of Acre was when Richard started tying blue leather thongs to the thighs of his Knights, and Acre was given over to the Venetians.

It seems the origins of St George's place in England started there. It also seems that the fervent and holy the wish to acquire Jerusalem for Christianity may have had commercial undertones. The Crusades were hostile takeovers of trade routes and the Cities that protected them.

White Gloves

Whether it was in the Levant during the Crusades, or later in France during the Hundred Years War, or during the Civil War, Venice was always there to lend a hand and make a killing. They were the experts in running a sea-based empire, what's technically known as a *thalassocracy*, and their expertise had a pedigree that is worth examining.

In the ancient world the Phoenicians had had outposts all round the Mediterranean. They came from what is now Lebanon, but had settled in North Africa, at Carthage, and had regular trade routes connecting Cyprus, Crete, Sicily and Sardinia.

They were the foremost traders in the ancient world, their network of ships and ports was at the heart of East Mediterranean culture, facilitating the exchange of goods and ideas, they became very rich, had too much gold but not enough steel.

Eventually the wealthy Phoenician sea-trade thalassocracy came up against the hungry, *tellurocracy* (land-based empire) of Rome, and got its arse handed to them.

The Roman victory over Carthage, in the Punic Wars, gave them dominion over the Mediterranean Sea. It also gave them the know-how to extend their Empire on land.

The Phoenicians were technologically superior to the Romans. One technique that surprised the Romans was a kind of Phoenician flat-pack furniture, they had created an ancient, weaponized, forerunner to Ikea.

The Phoenicians mass-produced their boats off-plan, using standardised masts, anchors, sails and rigging, every hull was made using the exact same number of planks of wood, which were all pre-cut and ready to assemble. This was much more efficient than building boats individually, and is an early example of the assembly-line process Henry Ford perfected.

Ships were the greatest engineering achievements of their day, they involved cutting edge technology and considerable risk. Phoenician manufacturing techniques pushed the boundaries of what was possible.

The Romans took this idea and ran with it.

For example, Roman legions would no longer have to drag their heavy artillery with them on long marches. Instead, they would take all the metal fixings and fittings needed to build a catapult, trebuchet or whatever, in a bag of bits, like the one you get from Ikea. They would then cut down trees to given measurements, and assemble their weapons using the bits they had brought.

Roman Soldiers discover the delights of flat-packs

This mass-production approach made the Roman war-machine much more efficient, literally more bang - and stab – for their buck.

The Phoenicians were master mathematicians and efficient manufacturers, their technology, used by the Romans, increased the range and power of their products beyond the dreams of any modern management consultant.

These methods were later adopted then adapted by the Venetians, who had learned them in Rome.

The Arsenal

In Venice there was a ship-building factory, called the Arsenal, which was the biggest manufacturing plant the world had ever seen. It employed about sixteen thousand people, covered over one hundred acres and became a hub of innovation in making both ships and weapons.

Once a ship had its hull, it was floated along a canal and worked on by specialised teams of engineers, riggers and carpenters. In 1320 the Arsenal was remade, and a new type of ship, the Grand Galley, was produced.

At its peak, the Arsenal could build one Galley a day, while elsewhere in Europe a single ship could take months.

By about 1450, Venice had a fleet of over three thousand ships, which dominated Mediterranean trade and made Venice rich. The Venetian state kept a monopoly in ship-building, they would lease the Galleys out to the highest bidder, but the state would retain ownership.

When Rome was overrun, in about the middle of the 5th century, some of its wealthier inhabitants had escaped and founded Venice.

By about 800A.D. Venice was a thriving commercial centre, by about 1200A.D. it had become a naval super-power and empire. The Venetian Gold Ducat was stamped with the name of the current Doge.

The Doge was the head of the group of families that owned and ran Venice. Their appointment was for life, but their power was limited.

One Doge tried to become a dictator and was publicly beheaded. There was a complex system put in place to prevent power falling into too few hands, this stability allowed business to thrive. They had learnt in Rome that an all-powerful Emperor was not good for business.

The distaste for a supreme ruler, above the law, has ancient roots, and found its expression in the City through the Whigs.

The potential profits from a single Venetian merchant voyage to the east could exceed 100%. This incredibly lucrative business drove some people mad, and over the years the corruption and decadence of Venice became legendary. They grew rich and wanted more, they would do anything for a ducat. This included slavery, war, genocide, anything you could think of, and worse.

They were experts.

They were also, coincidentally, the biggest bankers in Europe.

By the early fourteenth century, they had limited liability joint stock companies, markets for debt, mortgages, bankruptcy laws, double-entry accounting, deposit banking, and a world-famous currency.

All of which were necessary to manage long-distance trade. They constantly played different countries off against each other, for example, organising the pillaging of Christian Constantinople by the soldiers of the fourth Crusade in 1202.[59] This Crusade had meant to retake Jerusalem, but had been manipulated into killing their fellow religionists and looting the greatest city in Christendom.   The Venetians were willing to divide and conquer in ways that out-flanked people who had a moral compass.

They would do anything.

By 1508 the Venetians were so hated that the Kings of France, Spain, the Holy Roman Emperor, the Pope and the City states of Milan and Florence all ganged up to destroy them.

This was called the *League of Cambrai* and it marked the beginning of the end for the Venetian Empire.

On 27th April 1509, the Pope excommunicated the entire City.

I'm not clear what that meant for the thousands of slaves Venice traded in. Were they, as Venetian property, also damned?

What about the tourists? Did it mean every Venetian from the beginning of time to the end was dammed? It didn't really make sense to excommunicate a City, but it demonstrates the animosity they generated in Rome.

Venetian duplicity and greed slowly tore the fabric of their trade empire apart - they could not be trusted.

Venice declined as a Mediterranean and commercial power.

At about the same time ports in the Low Countries, and London, rose as global players, as transatlantic trade deepened and global exploration and exploitation developed. Expertise and cash from Venice came to London, and the City, especially the Lombard Bankers, prospered on a scale unmatched in history.

St George's, Bloomsbury – Lion and Unicorn fighting on the spire...

Chapter 8
The God of Money

In 1714, King George I, previously leader of a small German state with no real government experience, was crowned and the City had found its Doge. His head was stamped onto new coins, but his power as God-King was entirely symbolic.

To the Stuarts this would have been a mortal insult. Charles I had been beheaded because he refused to compromise his vision of Divine Right. But their time had passed.

The current incarnation of the infinite power of God on earth was a chubby bloke from Hanover.

He was *57th* in line to the throne by normal standards, the Tories had wanted a Stuart to rule, but the Whigs won out. London became the new Venice with stable government, a growing Navy, and, of course, lots and lots of bankers. The God of Money had found a new church.

The study of money is called numismatics and it is really the study of religion, of faith, as the two are inextricably and illuminatingly intertwined. There is no money if there are no shared values.

Money is something we pray for, worship and obey. It is an incarnation of the power of our collective imaginations.

Nowadays, if I have enough pictures of the Queen - notes - harnessing the shared values of my culture, I can do what I want: but there is always a limit. The amount of money I have is exactly the same as the amount of choice I have. Money is material freedom, is based on a shared understanding of value, and is decorated with signs and symbols to ensure you trust it.

This was also true in Babylon five thousand years ago. The system has not changed all that much. It is an ancient and powerful faith.

In Mesopotamia each City-state was built around a central temple to their local deity. The population were expected to make their offerings to the Temple, these were not voluntary, they were more like taxes. The Temple's store of wealth meant it was always the single richest entity in the City.

From the earliest times coins were struck with the names and faces of their leaders on one side, and an image of their god on the other.

These god-kings lent their power to the coins, to question the power of money was to question the whole power structure of the City. Religious beliefs and daily life reinforced each other, and people's faith in money was established.

In Ancient Egypt there were granaries where people had to take their crops to be stored. The presiding priests would weigh and measure what you brought in, in some cases they gave people receipts that could then be used to barter for other goods.

It seems there was ancient Egyptian paper money; Gold was too precious a medium for the ordinary people, and was the preserve of the super-rich. There were different currencies for different classes of people, with the poorest paid in set amounts of beer and bread.

There were forty-two *nomes* in Egypt, these were an ancient forerunner of the Parish Church.[60]

Each *nome* was a granary and temple to a local or national deity, it was the centre of civic and religious life and regulated the area's population. The *nomes* were dotted up and down the Nile, and roughly reflected population density, they popped up as the area became cultivated enough to produce a surplus.

Every *nome* had to produce more than it consumed, every god became greater than it was before. This was what defined an area as godly: it produced a surplus. The role of the depositories as the fore-runners of modern banks is worth reflecting on.

These state-run granaries are referred to in Genesis Chapter 41, the story of Joseph with his *'Technicolour Dream-Coat.'*

Joseph - Prophet of profits!

He interpreted a dream of Pharaoh's to mean there would be seven years of plenty followed by seven years of famine, so instructed everyone in Egypt to put food about 20% of their food into storage. Pharaoh was so pleased he called Joseph, *Zaphanath-Paaneah.* This translates as *'revealer of secrets'*, but would sound cool whatever it meant.

Joseph was hardly a benevolent figure however, when times got tough people had to buy back their own corn at inflated prices.

The Bible says some people had to sell their children into slavery in order to afford Joseph's stored grain.

The story clearly depicts the power of Egyptian grain-banking, which continued into the Christian era. The Bible, it seems, wants you to trust bankers, or at least obey them, be in awe of them, they can interpret your dream.

Joseph was a prophet of profit?

When Alexandria was founded in 331 B.C., the new Greek rulers of Egypt created a new series of state granaries.

You had to store all your food there, and this would cost you, the priests would decide how much they would take of your harvest as a fee for looking after it. This was obviously not a free society, it turned those in control of the granaries into the masters, and the general population into slaves. This centralised control enabled the rulers of Alexandria to become some of the richest people in the Ancient World.

In Rome, the Temple of Juno Moneta, the goddess of money, stood on the apex of the Arx, the innermost citadel of the imperial capital.

It was here that the gold coins for the Empire were struck, again with the images of their god-king, the emperor.

There's a story that a priestess of Juno Moneta foresaw the coming of Christ and told the first Emperor, Augustus.

He then had a vision of the Virgin Mary holding the Baby Jesus. This story seems to me to encrypt the money-makers reverence for Isis and Horus, the original Virgin and Holy Child. This story began being told in the early Christian era.

Perhaps it was created to associate Roman money with the faith that was to come. It directly links money, empire and religion, which is only appropriate.

That is the way Empires work, and what Hawksmoor tried to embody with his Churches.

The Venetian influence enables us to trace the origins of thalassocracy that now governs world trade, via the City, into the modern era. The Phoenicians taught the Romans, some left Rome and started Venice, the Venetians empowered the City of London. These traditions are at the secret heart of Empire, they are what make the imperial engine tick.

Having sketched out some of the considerations that would have been on his mind I want now to walk you through the churches and their parishes.

St George's Bloomsbury

Chapter 9
The Mind's Eye Tour

I'm going to take you on a tour of the six parishes where Hawksmoor's churches can be found, from Greenwich through Limehouse, Wapping, Spitalfields, the City and ending in Bloomsbury.

On the way I will be highlighting certain features of the churches and their parishes. This is to prepare you for what is to come, my suggestion for why Hawksmoor did what he did, what it meant for him.

I'm suggesting that each church can be understood through the character of the area they inhabit, this is my interpretation of their psychogeography.

Hawksmoor created buildings that were designed to last a thousand years and so define the type of place they inhabited using the silent language of architecture. If you understand this visual communication you understand that the poverty or prosperity of the different parishes is baked-in, part of the design.

This is best understood by looking at the churches and their parishes. It is possible to see all six in one afternoon.

Dickens described his writing as like 'streaky bacon', a slice of fat then a slither of meat, stacked up into a stripy rasher. This is something that Londoners get used to, emotionally as well as architecturally; you never quite know what's round the next corner.

One of the most compelling features of this route via these churches is the stark contrasts that you encounter. This is a great way to see and understand London.

Greenwich Observatory (Pic: Common Domain)

(1) -Greenwich

What better place is there to start a story than at the home of Space and Time?!

This place is the centre of the world: locations are marked by degrees East or West by virtue of their relationship to Greenwich. The web of lines of latitude and longitude seen on every map were spun from this spot.

This place stands on the edge of eternity, the midday sun – here - giving the definition of time, linking the earth to the heavens.

London, and later the whole world, knew the date and time that were set here.

The observatory is a kind of temple to a new religion, one that had begun in whispers, that now, in 1660s London, could proudly exclaim its commandments. Science, the mathematical analysis of natural phenomena, was blasting holes through the cultural fabric of Christendom.

Years before, Galileo had seen moons orbiting Jupiter, dispelling the myth that the Earth was at the centre of the Universe. He had been put under house arrest, and forbidden to look at the heavens again. This harsh treatment had scared some scientists into silence, others quietly made plans to move somewhere more hospitable.

In November 1660 Charles I gave his blessing to the Royal Society.

In England, sciences and technologies, especially lucrative ones, were not just welcome, they were given Royal approval.

The Society's motto remains – *Nullius In Verba* - take nobody's word for it - so by experiment and demonstration, not tradition, matters were to be settled. A radical step after millennia of religious dogma.

These Mathematicians considered themselves to be an Invisible College, spread out over Europe, often having to communicate in code, there were long-standing relationships through the exchange of ideas.

St Alphege's, Greenwich Church Street,

With the Royal Society, this secretive network had found a home.

It provided profit and pleasure all round. The Royal Observatory was one of the first fruits of this patronage. This building was the 17th century equivalent of the CERN particle accelerator today, it was a massive and expensive undertaking. Happily, it soon achieved famous results.

It was from this spot that Sir Nicholas Flamsteed, the Astronomer Royal, made the most accurate measurements yet taken of the moon's orbit. This data was then sent to Cambridge, where Sir Isaac Newton used it to establish Universal Gravitation.

This place is a temple to measurement and mathematical precision.

At 1 pm, since 1833, the red ball on top of the Observatory has dropped, signalling to all around the definition of the correct time. Before this time, on certain days of the year midday was signalled by raising a flag. Anyone in London with a telescope could set their clock by it.

This was common practice amongst the Parish Churches, whose bells would then ring out the phases of the day. By this simple mechanism order was enforced, every man woman and child knew exactly when to pray, when to work, when to go to bed.

There was a network of clocks across London, and their mechanical pulse drove the people of this town, the was no longer ruled by the rising and setting sun, or the seasons, there was a new master in town.

Greenwich Hill is my favourite place to see London. Beneath you are the regular, symmetrically placed, nicely proportioned buildings of the old Royal Naval Hospital. The emphasis is on *Royal*. This parish had enjoyed royal patronage for centuries, the old Greenwich palace had been a favourite of Henry VIII. Hawksmoor ensured this area remained suitably picturesque.

Hawksmoor called St Alphege's his 'stone cube', referring to the traditional cornerstone placed in the North East quarter of a building's foundations.

It is actually a massive stone cuboid, decorated with mock Roman Funeral Urns. This was a new Protestant Church, built as such, his churches would used as models for new churches all across the protestant world. Parish Churches under Rome were based around a crucifix floor-plan and natural proportions, but this was considered superstitious by Hawksmoor and Wren.

Each Parish Church was to be cuboid, not cruciform, and each would have a distinctive spire. In the days before street maps, distinctive buildings and pub signs were used to give directions. The planned net-work of churches would make each parish visible, discernable from a distance. God's church giving you directions and a sense of place.

The spire of St Alphege's can be seen from the river, its curvature and elegance emit a serenity, the clock face imposes regularity and exudes a calm reassuring authority.

All is as it should be. The interior is beautifully restored, with polished woods, a raised altar and intricate *composite* columns.

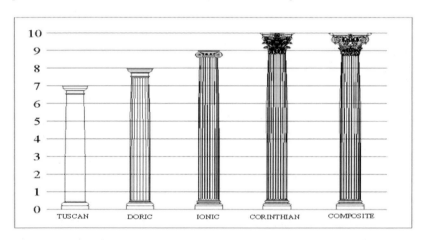

The use of this type of column tells us something.

In traditional architectural language, columns represent people, and there are different classes.
In Hawksmoor's 3 East-End Churches we will see plainer Tuscan style columns, this reflects the lower class of people who will frequent them.

St Alphege's Royal status is silently, subtly affirmed by the use of composite columns, and inequality is built in to the fabric of London.

From the 1670's the rebuilding of St Paul's Cathedral had been paid for by a tax on coal, by 1710 the building was almost finished.

That same year the roof of the old St Alphege's had collapsed, and the Parish asked for the money from the coal-tax to rebuild the church.

This proved to be exceptionally, maybe literally unbelievably, good timing all round.

St Alphege's needed to be enlarged to serve the Naval Hospital. It was, besides, a Royal Church, having been the site of the Baptism of Henry VIII in 1491. It was built on the spot where Archbishop Alphege had been martyred in 1012, having refused to let himself be ransomed by pirates.

Something had to be done to restore the church, and, luckily for Hawksmoor, in 1710 a new Tory government had just come into power. Hawksmoor was a direct beneficiary of Sacheverell's Sermon about False Brethren.

In 1711 the Tories passed the fifty Churches Act, the stated intention being to build fifty churches outside the City limits, especially in the east end.

Each Parish church acted as a hub for local governance, collecting taxes, establishing policing, dealing with local issues via the Parish Council. They also tended to your eternal soul and taught you how to avoid an eternity of torture and damnation.

The Tories intended the 50 Churches to stamp their authority, God's authority, onto the chaotic streets of London.

They sought to regulate and pacify the mob by imposing their vision on every citizen. Everyone had to go to church and be taught how to behave, the Tories wanted more churches to achieve greater obedience. The architect Vanbrugh, who started out as a set designer in the theatre, said these churches should be *'solemn and awful'*: looking at these buildings was meant to subdue your spirit and incline you to conformity.

Limehouse Fields Estate, E14

(2) - Limehouse

Having wandered down from Greenwich Hill and explored St Alphege's we need to cross the river to get to Limehouse.

Take the river-boat to Canary Wharf and you can see St Anne's from about a mile away. It is a massive statement of intent, its spire once housed the second highest clock tower in the country.

This clock used to chime every fifteen minutes and it was used to regulate the behaviour of some of the less motivated parishioners – you'd be given a job to do and get it done by the next bell, or else.

Limehouse was at the opposite end of the hierarchy to Greenwich.

It takes its name from the lime kilns that worked in this area, that made the air thick and caustic. This was an area where people used collected urine to tan leather, where much of the worst paid and least attractive work was done.

Later, the area became notorious for its Opium use, at one time it housed a huge Chinese community who worked on the docks.

Today, between Limehouse and Spitalfields the population is overwhelmingly Bangladeshi.

The borough of Tower Hamlets is one of the poorest areas in Europe, its where the City houses many of its cleaners, the street sweepers, the lesser functionaries that keep business going. The east is kept derelict and unattractive – cheap – so that the City can maintain a low cost work-force. This is town-planning.

The contrast between Greenwich and Limehouse is stark. Greenwich, with the Royal Park and Naval Hospital, The Observatory and Queen's House was, and is, fashionable and expensive. Limehouse, with its tanneries and hovels, pubs and brothels, has always offered a wholly less attractive prospect.

You arrive at Canary Wharf from the river-boat, and can go from the glitz of glass and steel, billion-pound mega-structures to the dire and

St. Anne's Church, Limehouse

drab communal housing of Three Colts Lane Estate in less than five minutes.

This contrast is easy to see, but when you're there you can feel it too, something in the air in Canary Wharf evaporates in Limehouse. Maybe it's hope? Optimism?

The area was a warren of poorly built one or two-storey shops and communal living houses.

The Parish was small but densely populated, Hawksmoor's St Anne's towers above everything even today, its sheer scale and massive bulk sending out a clear message to the docks and shops beneath.

Like all his Churches it was built of white Portland stone, which would set it apart from the dark brick housing about it. It is a massively imposing presence in the area, designed specifically to impress the locals with the power of God, commanding their obedience with silent might.

The spire is topped with pyramids, and they look a bit like massive candles, and the naval Ensign Flag flies under a shiny brass ball.

This device was used in signalling, a technique used first in Venice.

Messages would be conveyed by reflecting sunlight off a mirror and aimed at the spire.

Greenwich Hill would have been a perfect spot to do this: the sender would know the message was being delivered by seeing the metal ball lit up by the reflected light. This would have been for signalling in times of war, could have warned the parishioners in Limehouse of trouble spotted down river from Greenwich.

Presumably the message would then have been communicated to the City.

The church interior is very different from St Alphege's, there are no decorative columns, no intricate altar work, there is instead imposing scale and austere simplicity. The plain white stone makes the room feel eerie, it feels abandoned, under-populated, even when there are people inside. To have a look, I had to attend a Sunday service, the building is not open much, and the vicar was so pleased to see someone new it was embarrassing.

St Anne's massive bulk and imposing scale are now, almost hilariously, invisible from the street opposite.

Hawksmoor built the church to dominate the sky-line for miles around, but then someone, presumably a Whig, planted over twenty huge trees in the church grounds.

During the summer the leaves obscure the building nearly completely, although you can see St Anne's from a mile away on the river, across the street you can't. Someone deliberately obscured Hawksmoor's gargantuan edifice, its domination of the area artfully undermined.

St Anne's is also where you find Hawksmoor's pyramid, which was allegedly intended to be one of two to be put on the roof. The royal coat of arms on the third tier is far too small to have been visible from there, and it can't have been an afterthought, you couldn't have just added it on, it sticks out.

The engraving about the *Wisdom of Solomon* could have been added later, of course, but I think this was not what Hawksmoor was up to. The pyramid was not an accident.

What it was, was a ten-ton *UP YOURS!* if you know the context.

By the time St Anne's was being built the Stuarts were off the throne, they had tried to regain it, starting in Scotland in 1715, and they tried again in 1745. They always failed.

But a Scottish style Freemason like Hawksmoor would have had severe reservations about the legitimacy of the new Hanoverian King, George I.

Many Scottish Freemasons, Tories and aristocrats wanted the Stuarts back. Hawksmoor placed the *Wisdom of Solomon* above the Royal Crest, it seems like a declaration of his priorities, of his loyalties. His creed was more important to him than his new King, who represented unwelcome change.

Hawksmoor worked to engrain his vision for London in on the fabric of its sacred spaces.

Each one lights up its parish with a beacon of Tory values. St Anne's stands like a sentinel over the Thames, the variations of the tides subdued by the regularity of the clock.

As returning ships went passed Greenwich, north up the Thames sailors would see her and know they were home, she was the first of London they saw when they arrived, and the last when they left, a guardian of the boundary.

Rotherhithe converted wharfs from the opposite bank
Pen & Watercolour – KRB 2000

(3) - Wapping

The journey from Limehouse to Wapping is not pretty.

This is off the tourist trail. No postcards are available. No romantic comedies have been set here by Hollywood producers, and for good reason. These two Parishes have long been synonymous with crime and depravation, even as much of London has been modernised, they remain doggedly dreary and unwelcoming.

I'd recommend taking the D3 bus from outside St Anne's to Tobacco Dock, which is just south of St George's In The East.

This route will take you through much of Wapping, with many of the Ware-Houses-At-River-Front (W.H.A.R.F.s) having been converted into flats that over look the river.

Across the street from the river-side apartments you'll see a lot of less luxurious social housing. *Streaky Bacon* style, on one side of the street a flat can cost millions, on the other side the same amount of space will cost you next to nothing.

These luxury flats were not part of Hawksmoor's design, he knew Wapping for what it was back then. The heart of the Docks: a frenzied, violent and lawless place.

The East End was already poor and unloved, the sort of area immigrants came to then moved out of as soon as they could. Hawksmoor's Churches cemented this reality, and reflect it back on itself, they are ghostly and austere, buildings made to make you squirm, to make you feel small and powerless.

Execution Dock lay in Wapping, it was, as its name suggested, where breaches of Maritime law were punished. The bodies of executed pirates were left to hang in metal cages over the river to remind all concerned what they could expect if they disobeyed. Crimes committed at sea anywhere in the world were punished here. The cages were a symbol of the Law's authority over the Sea.

St George In The East Church, Cannon Street Road, E1

Wapping and the Docks were, in some senses, the kernel of the nut that Hawksmoor was trying to crack. It was here that lawlessness, which was Godlessness, derived. There was no taming the docks, no taming the ceaseless growth in trade that threatened the old settled agriculture.

The Docks were insatiable, eating ships up then spitting them out again, emptied and filled, mended and tended. Sailors from North Africa, India and America arrived, bringing more and more diversity and novelty with them.

The profusion of languages, the increasingly exotic goods, the plants, animals and people from all over the world that were brought to London knew no limits. If something was unknown to London, London wanted to know about it.

Most importantly, London would pay the price to get it.

The demand for novelty snow-balled, as it snow-balls today. How do you control a beast that gets hungrier and stronger every time you feed it? The demands for goods and services, for novel excitement were a threat, as they a still are today.

Hawksmoor's answer was brutal.

A thousand-ton, thousand-year testimonial in stone to *Might is Right.* He and his friends were determined to impose order on chaos and check the power of trade and commerce.

'St George's In The East' is the most barefacedly brutal of his churches, it looks to me more like a castle than a place of worship.

It is placed on the high-ground to the north of Tobacco Docks, and, like St Anne's, would have dominated the sky-line for miles around. It is a crude expression of raw power and a warning to the lawless and ungodly. This church does not represent a gentle, forgiving, creator that dies for our sins.

This is more like the God that sent down Fire and Brimstone on the disobedient.

Tobacco Dock was situated right under the church for a reason.

Each commodity had a designated dock to handle those goods with specialist equipment, the weighing and measuring were tightly regulated.

Some docks were more prone to theft and violence than others, and Tobacco was one commodity that people would fight over. Putting the dock and church side by side highlights the function of Hawksmoor's churches, like stage sets they were designed to evoke emotional responses, ones so subtle the Dockers wouldn't notice.

They'd just obey, because they felt God was watching.

When the Nazis dropped a bomb on St George's during World War Two, Hawksmoor's God didn't bat an eyelid. From the outside the church seems untouched, the Nazis may have been tough, but Hawksmoor's God was tougher. This was the kind of God, he must have felt, that Wapping needed.

While Limehouse was unattractive, Wapping was positively dangerous.

St George's In The East typifies the immense power of Hawksmoor's churches, they are built with walls up to three foot thick, some of their features are brutal in their effect, they look intimidating.

The strange towers that he built on the roof here would, coincidentally, have been perfect 'roosts' for marksmen to fire from. A few well-placed soldiers could have rendered the parish grounds a killing zone, should the need ever have arisen.

This idea of God looking down on you, just like the Church looks over the Docks, was the inspiration for a technique Wren had used in some of his City Churches, and Hawksmoor used here. Above some of the doors are small elliptical windows, called 'oculus windows'. They create eye-shaped beams of light that penetrate the body of the church, intimating to the congregation that God could see right through them.

The spire is topped with eight mock funerary urns, the whole thing seems to reach upwards, to loom over you like a bouncer.

The effect is definitely reminiscent of a castle; it emanates a muscular stoicism. The interior was rebuilt in the 1960's, the roof rebuilt to cover most of the original nave, but not all. There is now an open courtyard between the spire and the body of the church. Here you can see how little damage the Nazi bomb did to the fabric of the building.

They destroyed the roof but the walls didn't bat an eyelid.

Wapping was synonymous with violence and depravity. In the 1980's Rupert Murdoch moved some of his newspapers there. In the 1930s there was the battle of Cable Street, when Moseley's Black-shirts were trying to intimidate the local immigrant population, which was mainly Jewish at that time.

You need to walk a few hundred yards north until you hit Whitechapel High Street, it is about a mile to Spitalfields Parish. I suggest you wander through the back streets a bit. You'll see poverty and deprivation as bad as anywhere else in Europe while being less than a mile from the richest place on Earth. London is about to change from poverty-trap to rich man's play-ground.

Inside Spitalfields market 2003

Photograph © Christine Matthews
https://www.geograph.org.uk/profile/1777

(4) - Spitalfields

Spitalfields is right on the edge of the City, it was a place as synonymous with poverty as Wapping was with violence.

Not that there wasn't violence, the murder of five prostitutes ascribed to *Jack The Ripper*, occurred within sight of Hawksmoor's church. There was crime and gambling and prostitution and drugs, and this made the area a bit of a temptation for many of the City Gents.

Now there are the Gentlemen's Clubs where Brothels used to be, there are furtive exchanges between suits and shell-suits where the drug dens used to be: many things remain the same.

On the corner of Fournier Street and Brick Lane there is a building that was originally built as a Protestant Church for the Huguenot's, religious refugees from France in the 17th century.

The same building was later taken over by East European Jews, fleeing the pogroms in the 19th century. For the last fifty years or so it has been a mosque for the local Bangladeshi community, some of whom first arrived in the area in the 1680s.

This building is, apparently, the only one in the world outside of Jerusalem to be have been used for all three Abrahamic faiths. I was taught this by Marge Hewitson, a Jewish lady working in a Christian school full of Muslim kids.

Spitalfields was a market, and probably one of the most cosmopolitan places in the world. It stood at the entrance to the richest, most powerful City in the world, goods and people from every corner of the globe would make their way there. The variety was pretty much impossible to police, so the area was left to its own devices, neglected.

Its central location and cheap rents have made it fashionable now, gentrification is just the latest way Spitalfields has experienced change. It is a place in motion, a meeting-point.

Christ Church Spitalfields,

At 202 feet, the spire at Christchurch is the tallest and most famous of all Hawksmoor's churches.

This is only natural, his other churches are dedicated to St Alphege, St Anne, St George, St Mary, and another to St George, but the church at Spitalfields name drops the main man, Jesus Christ.

Christchurch is the most famous of Hawksmoor's Churches for a reason.

Looking at it, from a distance or up close, it is unlike anything built before or since. There is a technical reason for this, as prototypes for a new religion, the Parish Churches Hawksmoor built for the Protestant faith were deliberately different.

The Old Cross-shaped floor plan of Catholic Churches was ruled out as superstitious, as was the use of the Fibonacci Series, a number pattern that had been integral to defining a sense of proportion in a building.

Wren considered this thinking backward, beauty was an impression made by matter on the eye, not something inherent. Wren and Hawksmoor used drawings and model-making to experiment with design ideas, their own version of the scientific method, rather than relying on tradition.

The era when Hawksmoor built his churches, 1711-35, started under Tory rule, but this only lasted till 1713, and the rest of the century belonged to the Whigs. Hawksmoor's churches were criticized by Whigs before they were even finished. Palladian architecture from Venice had become fashionable, this style reincorporated Fibonacci, and Hawksmoor was called out-dated by the Whigs after about 1720.

Spitalfield's spire looks a bit like a KKK headdress to me, it leers imposingly over you if you stand too close. The massive cubes of stone that support the pillars cry out with solidity and permanence. This God is no pushover.

The huge, plain, *Tuscan* pillars communicate brute strength to the brute community they serve. Gone are the decorative embellishments of older catholic churches, Christchurch is full of clean lines and sharp angles, it is a bulky beast. It looks unnatural because the proportions of the parts to the whole are not natural.

One feature of the Church was the tunnel built as an escape route, should the Parish Council need to escape.

As mentioned in Chapter 3 this was how I first got interested in the churches.

It taught me a lot about how these churches were viewed by those creating them. They were an imposition of Tory values like duty and obedience on an area of wild diversity.

They were redoubts of civility and godliness in a place of sin and debauchery.

They were stone signals that silently demanded conformity, they were there to tell you what to do, how to feel, who you were meant to be. This attitude is almost colonial, the churches were going to settle a barbarous place, whether the natives liked it or not. So they needed an escape tunnel in case the natives turned on them and rejected their version of heaven.

The Church faces west, and in the evening the whole front of it lights up at about the time workers would have been returning home to the East End. The view of it down Brushfield Street, which links the Church to the City, is one of Hawksmoor's greatest successes.

Whether you're aware of it or not, Christchurch defines your sense of space. When I lived in Whitechapel it became, as you bear witness, a bit of an obsession.

As the Church is dedicated to Christ it is not surprising it has a special place in the arrangement of Hawksmoor's Churches across London.

It is the northernmost, with Wapping and Limehouse to the East, the City and Bloomsbury churches to the West. It is the jewel in the crown of the row of five churches he strung out on the north side of the Thames, in and around the City proper. It is the heart of the system, the meeting point, the fulcrum, where, you could say, heaven comes down to earth.

Sometimes, Christopher Wren would sign his name 'Xtopher', or similar.

I learnt that's because the symbol 'X' is the sound 'Chi' in Greek, so it was a short-hand for him, and that's why 'Xmas' is a thing. 'X' as a symbol was used by Plato to describe how heaven and earth meet, there's a upper 'V' pointing down, and a lower one pointing up, and like an hourglass, there's a point where these two halves meet.

This is part of the symbolism of Christ, whether you look at an 'X' or a regular crucifix you are looking at a symbol of disparate elements coming together. He is part God but part man, of this world and the next, a bridge-builder between the two, inviting everyone to pass through him to eternity.

Royal Exchange with City of London in background
Photograph © Freeman 2019
C.C. - https://www.geograph.org.uk/profile/117712

(5) - The City

The route from Christchurch to St Mary Woolnoth, from Spitalfields into the City is one of my favourite parts of this journey.

You can walk straight down Brushfield Street onto Bishopsgate, but that, in my view, is a mistake.

Taking a left and weaving your way through the back streets you find Catherine Wheel Alley, which narrows down to about two feet across before opening out onto Bishopsgate. Suddenly you are within a few yards of some of the grandest, most modern and brash buildings in the City.

It feels like an initiation.

Huge new towers have been built here since the Financial Crisis of 2008.

It seems that the same forces that cut family budgets and left millions of people worse off have raised these mega-structures. The economic cycle of boom and bust is perhaps better understood as seasons of growth and harvest. There has been a consolidation of wealth into the hands of the few.

George Soros noted it was the Sovereign Wealth Funds that seemed to do all the buying post 2008.

The lack of cash in 2008 saw the stock prices of many firms drop catastrophically.

For example, Bear Sterns, a bank, was valued at about $80 billion one day, a week later it was bought for less than $8 billion.

That $72 billion difference was lost, somehow, somewhere. The difference between the probably inflated initial price, and the probably devalued sale price meant someone probably made about a $40 billion profit. Harvest time.

Sovereign wealth funds are huge private fortunes, deriving from oil or other commodities in countries that don't share their wealth around, they hoard it at the top. They own nearly everything, using trust funds, located off-shore, which allow them to avoid tax, to buy and sell in enormous deals.

Their decisions are much more influential than those of our elected representatives. Many politicians will have worked for them before entering public life, and return to them after.

Britain governs thirteen of the world's top twenty tax-havens, managing assets estimated at between thirteen and thirty trillion dollars.

No one knows how much exactly because this is exactly what trust funds do, they make it impossible to work out what they are, and who benefits. These sovereign wealth funds, managed through trust funds by City firms, are the most powerful forces on earth.

In 2016 the European Union announced it would clamp down on tax-havens, so Britain's then Prime Minister, David Cameron, tried to get exemptions for trust funds managed in the City. This failed, and he called the Brexit referendum, lost and resigned. This was probably not an accident.

His father, Ian, was one of the pioneers of placing funds off-shore, something the Thatcher Government in the 1980's had facilitated.

Cameron banned the EU from 'interfering' with the referendum, making it very difficult for the pro-EU lobby to match the propaganda of the Trust-Fund owned media. It is inconceivable that David Cameron will not have benefited from this.

He saved the richest people in the world from billions, maybe even trillions, in taxes in the decades to come.

St Mary Church, Woolnoth
Corner of Lombard Street and King William Street, EC3

Even if you stand right outside St Mary Woolnoth you could still miss it, it is not as imposing as Christchurch, was built with a different purpose in mind.

The layered stone effect on the exterior walls reflects Hawksmoor's respect for history.

An ancient temple to Mithras had been discovered nearby, the layers of earth shared their hidden secrets. Hawksmoor reflected this in the layers of stone, and it was a popular idea, copied by many of the buildings in the City. Some of the Headquarters of the most powerful companies in the world were built to reflect and respect his church, it set the architectural standard at the heart of the Empire.

As the Parish Church of the Governor of the Bank of England and the Lord Mayor it is a place of quiet reflection, and deep thought. It is worth noting that Hawksmoor built the Church under the auspices of the 50 Churches Act.

The Act was supposed to build churches outside the City, for the benefit and education of the poor.

Perhaps this is the richest Parish in the world, home to the Bank of England, Lombard Street and the Royal Exchange. The church, however, was rebuilt, in High Tory fashion, using money allocated for the poor.

Today they would probably use Lottery Money.

This place was where some of the most important decisions in the world were made, here the elite of the City could discuss the business of the day and contemplate eternity.

It is decorated in a deliberately masonic fashion, with twisting columns either side of the altar, the interior is a cube within a cube. In Vaughan Hart's book about Hawksmoor he refers to this church as the culmination of his fascination with the Temple of Solomon.

From the outside it is strangely unimpressive compared to his other churches, much more discreet.

The name is strange and allegedly derived from 'will-not-marry'.

The Mary will-not-marry church. So, St Mary is a virgin, or a spinster perhaps?

She lacks the ostentatious scale of the other churches, is muted and downbeat.

She is an almost imperceptible presence in the heart of the City, overshadowed by the massive Bank of England, the opulent Mansion House and The Old Exchange, now one of the most expensive shopping centres in the world.

She does not ask for your attention, seems disposed to being ignored, so she can get on with her business: weighing, measuring and harvesting the world. St Mary Woolnoth exists at centre of Empire, quietly watching as the institutions around her make conquest after conquest.

The last stop on our journey awaits, in Bloomsbury Hawksmoor's weirdest church, St George's.

A number 15 bus will take you there; away, to the place of wonders, the Elysium that was London's fantastically fashionable and prodigiously prosperous West End.

British Museum
Source: Section from original picture by "Ham" - Own work, CC BY-SA 3.0
(Picture has been darkened for this book)

(6) - Bloomsbury

Our journey began in the detached heights of Greenwich Hill, above it all and aloof, St Alphege's was Hawksmoor's stone cube, or foundation.

We were bade welcome to the City by St Anne's, the graceful sentinel of Limehouse, whose clock rang out every fifteen minutes, driving the pace of the day.

In Wapping we found the docks were overlooked by the battlements of St George's-In-The-East, looming large over the crime and chaos. Christchurch, and the markets, is the meeting point between heaven and earth, the pristine order of the City is confronted by the revels and rebels of the East End.

At St Mary Woolnoth we saw a quiet wisdom, a subtle logic at play, grander designs overshadow her, which allows her to get on with her business undisturbed.

Finally, we're in Bloomsbury.

The Parish was fashionable, Bloomsbury Square was built by the Earl of Southampton in the early 1660's, and was the first of the famous Squares of the West End, including Berkeley, Belgrave, Grosvenor and Fitzroy.

All this property development out West, the squares, was for the great and the good to enjoy. The East would house the least fortunate, and never the twain should meet. Bloomsbury epitomised wealth and success, the fruits of Empire were planted here, in bricks and mortar, houses, shops, restaurants and theatres, and, of course, in the British Museum.

When conceived, the British Museum was probably the most ambitious institution in the world.

It was designed and built as a *Universal Museum*, it would contain everything, without limits, it would absorb the content of the world, categorise and catalogue them. Every animal, mineral, vegetable - even fungi - and every country and culture, past or present, would be represented.

St. George's Church, Bloomsbury

At the centre of the Museum was the British Library, which would contain every book ever written. The recorded knowledge, the memory of the Empire, all under one roof.

A mate at school played a trick on me once, he told me some of his family were coming to stay with him so they could see something that was stolen from just down the road from where they lived.

He told me the thieves had put the items on display and anyone could come see them, and while they were in London his family thought they should go and have a look. His family had fled the 1978 Revolution in Iran, his relatives lived near where some of the Persian carvings in the British Museum were from.

Looked at this way, you could say the whole Museum is an offensively ostentatious display cabinet for pirated goods, an industrialised thieves' gallery. The security around the Museum suggests they think people out there are thinking that way.

Some of the greatest treasures of the Museum are wanted back because they were stolen. No one ever took something they thought worthless to the Museum, they took valuable items, some more so than others.

The Museum was designed to bring greater order to knowledge through thorough systems of quantification and categorisation, it was always better if the item could be given a number, a date, a value, and at very least a name, a label by which it could be related to the whole realm of scientific enquiry.

Anything that the Navy or the Companies discovered anywhere in the world would come back to Bloomsbury to be assessed. It became a fascinating place to live and has a long association with collectors, antiquaries, strange bookshops and weird and wonderful clubs.

Stuff went down in Bloomsbury after sunset.

Finally, we have arrived at our destination, the culmination of our journey through space, time and mind.

St. George's looks nothing like a church, its Greek looking front, with pretty Corinthian capitals on the pillars, the steeple which sticks out a mile, literally, is the strangest I've ever seen.

Lion and Unicorn Fighting on a Church Spire, St George's Bloomsbury

In Bloomsbury, in London's West End, we will experience triumph and glory, even victory over death, by contemplating the most ostentatiously weird church in London, St George's. Hawksmoor copied the most famous celebration of death in the world, the Mausoleum at Halicarnassus, and stuck at the top of the church, this was crowned with a statute of George I, whom the City Big-Whigs had decided would be king.

The Lion and the Unicorn fighting on the steps of the pyramid represent the struggle for the monarchy between the houses of Stuart the unicorn and Hanover the lion. Was Hawksmoor trying to be satirical, on a church, by using an image of the king? It was still possible the Stuarts would return again to the Throne, they gave it a go but the City faction always proved too powerful for them.

> *The Lion and the Unicorn*
> *Were fighting for the crown*
> *The Lion beat the Unicorn*
> *All around town.*

The original statues were actually chipped off and destroyed in the 19th Century, they were called "rude ornaments", by someone with nothing better to do.

The installation of the replacement includes a weird story, one that nicely sums up the place.

Before the Unicorns horn was put into place all the local school children were encouraged to join hands and form a ring around the church. The horn was then passed around the circle and then handed to H.R.H. Prince Michael, Duke Of Kent, who was, coincidentally, the highest-ranking Freemason in the country.

St George's is orientated North-South not East-West like most churches. The '50 Churches Act' actually stated the churches should lie East-West, but Hawksmoor ignored them.

He spent a fortune for the land, paying £1,000 to Lady Russell, who had fallen on hard times since James II had had her Whig husband executed in 1683.

As mentioned in Chapter 3, Hawksmoor supervised his apprentice, John James, in the construction of St John's Horsleydown in Bermondsey. Hawksmoor bought the land, and designed the spire, but did not consider this church to be as important to his scheme as the rest. It was a second tier building, a placeholder built with less expensive materials, paid for by the fifty Churches Act.

It was demolished after sustaining structural damage in World War II.

Some things have changed since Hawksmoor's day, but many remain the same.

As the sun rises in the East and falls in the West, so the gold of the City comes in from the East, via the Thames and the riches of trade, and takes root in the West, in the great houses of the fashionable squares.

This money, the profit of Empire, was then sent back East, and reinvested in the continued progress and prosperity of business. A profitable circuit was established.

This is the tour of London, the route through his churches that you need to see for yourself if you really want to understand Hawksmoor's work.

It takes you through the streaky bacon of London's variegated Parishes, rich and poor nestled next to each other for maximum profit. Profit was the glory of God, his bounty, Hawksmoor's vision of Christ will show us what he believed.

His churches are a sermon in stone: here cometh the lesson.

St John Horsleydown, Bermondsey

Temple of Solomon
Section of a modern interpretation by Wu Mingren
(Creative Commons)

Chapter 10
Mind Maps

To try to understand what Hawksmoor was doing I had to try and understand his perspective, how he viewed the world: his mind-map or imaginative frame. This obviously included his loyalty to the Stuarts generally and Sir Christopher Wren in particular.

Hawksmoor can be reasonably described as a Tory, a Unicorn, a Scottish Freemason, and as believing in Divine Right kingship.

Hawksmoor's training by Wren would have been more than just practical, it would have included faith, politics, aesthetics and philosophy; as we will see an architect was supposed to be the ultimate expression of humanity's creative power. God was an architect.

Freemasonry as practised by Hawksmoor may have had very little in common with the organisation that exists today. It is very hard to say what exactly he believed.

However, the rites of modern Freemasonry are well known, they focus on the Temple of Solomon and its architect, Hiram Abiff. Why anyone would bother with this sort of thing is the question I asked myself – what could the benefit be?

What can be said with some certainty is that Freemasonry was a branch of a larger 'esoteric' or 'occult' tradition that circulated throughout Europe during and after the Renaissance. This was given various names, for example, Hermeticism, Alchemy, and Rosicrucianism, all of which denoted different variations on the same broad themes.

The Roman church consistently persecuted these 'occult' or 'esoteric' practices as they emphasized a personal growth and reflection, rather than communal shared values.

These philosophical similarities are a good place to start to understand Hawksmoor's imagination, as they formed the historical background from which modern Freemasonry emerged.

The original, operative side of Freemasonry, that version which was practised by actual builders, clearly involved a lot of oral teaching.

In the Middle Ages some of the mathematical and engineering skills possessed by Freemasons, as demonstrated in the Gothic Cathedrals they built, were considered by the Church as dangerous, even satanic. Masons would have to be very cautious about who they shared their knowledge with, so they rarely wrote things down.

Lessons in maths and geometry would have been practical and given by master to apprentice in an ad hoc manner, there was no written curriculum. The hand-shakes and pass-words were used to identify a fellow mason, to protect themselves from infiltration and possible accusations of devilry.

It seems obvious that Masons would study geometry, and Euclid's work 'The Elements' would be an obvious place to start. This book was written in Alexandria in about 300B.C. The 37th Proposition in the Elements describes what we're taught as Pythagoras' Theorem and Freemasons held this in some awe.

Creating buildings of the size and beauty of the Gothic Cathedrals shows the working masons that roamed Europe had clearly developed incredible engineering skills, this underpinned by their understanding of geometry. With just a ruler and a compass some of these masons had the imaginative power to create incredible complex buildings with scientific precision.

As discussed previously this 'Irish' tradition of operative masons was joined by 'Scottish' freemasonry which was more speculative and philosophical, and seemed to be centred on the Stuart court.

Freemasonry as it was understood in Hawksmoor's time was a blend of operative terminology and practices from real builders, and the more speculative and philosophical aspects of the European 'esoteric' and 'occult' traditions.

For the purpose of this narrative it is important to look a little closer at the words 'esoteric' and 'occult' and tease out what they actually mean.

Esoteric means *secret*, occult means *hidden from sight*; so they involved secret and hidden practices, but what does this mean on a practical level?

Broadly they refer to what today we would call personal development or psychology. People would practice their 'art' and their mind would be changed by it, the aspiration usually being to get closer to God, to understand more of Creation by trying to imitate its workings.

An 'occult' student would create mandalas, or meditative images, recite prayers, create potions and or cast 'spells' to try to bring his or her mind closer to God.

The impact of these practices was 'occult' because the adept, on achieving some kind progress, would look the same as he or she did before, but something 'hidden' had changed.

Successful practice would refine the mind, in much the same way as meditation does. Just like some in the Christian tradition today consider yoga and meditation as dangerous or even Satanic, so did the Roman Church, and for the same reason: they could not control it.

The Church repeatedly persecuted esoteric practices; they offered a route to personal empowerment that undermined the church's ability to herd their flock. Imagine if the sheep all became lions and no longer needed their shepherd.

Clearly a lot of the esoteric tradition was based on superstitions that we would no longer entertain today, but that isn't to say it was all a waste of time.

So although it is impossible to know what exactly was going on in Hawksmoor's head I would argue it was reasonable to assume his practices included two techniques that throw some light on how he was thinking; I'm calling these the Science of Memory and Mind-Maps, and as you'll see these were often connected.

This subject is described in enormous detail in Frances Yates' book, The Art of Memory. I refer the interested reader to that amazing book.[61]

The Science Of Memory.

In the Book, Phaedrus, by Plato, there is a story about the Egyptian god Thoth, who had just invented letters, showing them to the Pharaoh Thamus.

"This invention, O king," said Thoth, *"will make the Egyptians wiser and will improve their memories; for it is an elixir of memory and wisdom that I have discovered."*

But Thamus replied, *"Most ingenious Thoth... you, who are the father of letters, have been led by your affection to ascribe to them a power the opposite of that which they really possess.*

For this invention will produce forgetfulness in the minds of those who learn to use it, because they will not practice their memory. Their trust in writing, produced by external characters which are no part of themselves, will discourage the use of their own memory within them".

In this tradition written language was viewed with suspicion, it took people's attention away from their perfectible soul and out toward a corrupting world. The very act of writing something down could corrupt it. The written word, from this perspective, can become a false idol, something that will cloud your vision of the truth.

The memory was the repository of wisdom and truth, things that you could only experience esoterically. Truth and wisdom could not be put into words; to try to do so was a form of blasphemy.

This Oral tradition in Egypt kept stories alive for millennia without needing to write them down. These stories could only become dogma by being written, made fixed and external. This was to be avoided.

Written language also made the brain lazy, removing the need for people to work on their memory.

The impact of this was felt all over Europe after the invention of the printing press: normal people who had had to remember huge stories and poems almost word-for-word no longer needed to, and very soon people's working memories atrophied as they were not needed or worked, not in constant use.

This impact of the written word upon the working memory is profound, and it forced some people in the Ancient World to do something about it.

Their solution was the 'Science of Memory', this was a set of techniques used to build and improve the memory. Memory is like a muscle that can be trained, and in doing so esoterically empowers the practitioner, and it all started at a dinner party.

The story goes a poet called Simonides was asked to entertain the guests at a wedding feast. He told them a story about 'Castor and Pollox', two heroic twins. When he asked for payment the host of the party said he'd only pay half Simonides' fee; he should collect the other half from the legendary twins.

Shortly after this Simonides was informed that two men were asking to see him outside and he left the host and others sitting at the table. While he was away the roof collapsed, killing all the other guests and mangling their bodies beyond recognition.

Simonides was able to tell the dead guests' relatives which guest was which by remembering where they sat at the table, and so reunited relatives with their loved ones' bodies.

It was the locations of the guests that had enabled Simonides to remember who was who, by location memory could be enhanced.

This story was told in the context of learning rhetoric, the ability to deliver powerful and persuasive speeches, as it was taught to the Greek and Roman aristocrats. Part of the art of rhetoric was this 'Science of Memory', which would enable the speaker to recall his narrative with incredible precision. Skilled rhetoricians could repeat hours-long speeches almost word for word.

Location, Location, Location

The fact that the guests had been seated in a particular order had enabled Simonides to remember who they were. This insight must have been the reason the story was invented, to communicate this fact. It was this use of locations that was then formalised into a teaching method.

The students were encouraged to visualise a place they knew well, this place should consist of several distinct areas that adjoin each other, and the student would walk through these places in a chosen order in their mind's eye.

The imaginary journey through this real location, with its series of discrete places visited in order became the mental page on which the speech would be written.

The 'text' consisted of a series of images that the student would put in place around their chosen location, more of this soon.

The clear picture of the location was paramount and it is easy to imagine students starting out with smaller buildings in mind, perhaps their homes. These small familiar places with well known attributes would given the student maybe ten or twelve separate *loci*.

With practice, however, they would be able to advance to more complex places, temples, theatres, perhaps even towns. These would afford the orator dozens, maybe even hundreds of places to insert the visual prompts they created.

It is easy to imagine that with practice the students mental 'work-space' was enlarged, allowing them to synthesis more and more information. Ordering their thoughts gave their memories greater capacity, and some orators were famous for being able to recite for hours on end.

Some teachers recommended marking every 5th locus, to help the student navigate their increasingly complex circuit, these markers would act as landmarks. Whatever image was place in the fifth place could be topped by a golden hand, the tenth place topped by a golden image of a friend called 'Decimus', at the fifteenth place Decimus with a golden hand, and so on.

The idea was that students should be able to journey through the memory place starting in any location and traveling in either direction along their route. This enabled the students to recall information as required with great facility.

Other features of a good location have a 'goldilocks', moderate, quality: the places should not be crowded; of medium size, not too big or small; well lit – neither dark nor too bright; evenly spaced apart from each other, and as mentioned above consisting of distinct areas: *a Colonnade, a Pond, a Recess*, and so on. All these techniques were found to enhance the mind's ability to create ordered thought.

Some teachers preferred to use exclusively real places for the setting of this mental exercise. Well known buildings of which the student had first hand experience had obvious advantages, one simply had to remember what the place was like.

Others, however, started to advocate for imaginary places being used. These places, it was argued, could be perfected to facilitate optimal efficiency, some argued these imaginative spaces were free of any constraint that might make remembering more difficult.

The extra work involved in creating an imaginative space was worth the effort, according to their advocates.

Later, the strict use of real places and items was called the 'square art', the use of fictitious locations and objects, the 'round art' and we'll return to this distinction later.

Iconic Art

The students of the Science of Memory would use their journey around their location as a way of ordering their thoughts. They would place images in the separate loci on their journey, each image was created to remind them of that particular part of their speech.

For example, to remember the story of Simonides the student might put an image of a table surmounted by heroic twins in the their imaginary *Colonnade*. This would remind them of the dinner-party and the story Simonides told.

In the next locus, the student's *Pond*, Simonides talking to the twins outside.

In the student's imaginary *Recess* the table could be broken and covered with distinct blotches of blood.

This is my attempt at creating images, a student of the Art of Memory would, I'm sure, do much better, but I hope you get the idea – you put images into the loci along your imaginative journey around the real building.

Advice for how to make effective images from a Roman teaching book, known as *Ad Herennium*, makes the psychological subtlety and insight involved in this practice clear.

"Now Nature herself advises us what we should do.

When we in every day life see things that are petty, ordinary and banal, we generally fail to remember them... But if we see something exceptionally base, dishonourable, unusual, great, unbelievable, or ridiculous, that we are likely to remember for a long time...

A sunrise, the sun's course, a sunset are marvellous to no one as they occur daily. But solar eclipses are a source of wonder because they occur seldom...Thus nature shows that she is not aroused by the common ordinary event, but is moved by the new or striking occurrence.

Let art, then, imitate nature, find what she desires, and follow as she directs... We ought then, to set up images of a kind that adhere longest in memory. And we shall do so if we establish similitudes as striking as possible..." [62]

Active, striking, shocking images were best as they were easy to remember.

These images could be used in a range of ways, for example, placing a rusty anchor to literally remind you that the navy was in need of repair. Other images rely on puns, if you placed a 'W' in front of the rusty anchor, you might be reminding yourself of the idiots in charge of the navy.

I invite you to imagine a locus where a Whale is secreting oil, this drips on to some beef, which is hanging from a Hook.

Whale Oil Beef Hooked!

Puns and visual cues used in Roman times included their gods and heroes, images and ideas already imbued with meaning that could be modified then be placed into the loci.

An image of Mars treading on the neck of Pharaoh would remind the orator that Rome had defeated Egypt.

An image of Venus grown fat could prompt the idea that love in Rome had become a decadent folly, and so on.

The famous Roman orator Cicero summarised the Art of Memory, he said, *"one must employ a large number of places which must be well lighted, clearly set out in order, at moderate intervals apart; and images which are active, sharply defined, unusual, and which have the power of speedily encountering and penetrating the psyche"*.[63]

Cicero later defined virtue as *"a habit of mind in harmony with reason and the order of nature"*. Someone's 'virtue' may not be self-evident but practice can *"undoubtedly summon it forth if it is in hiding"*.[64]

Virtue, he says, consisted of four parts, Prudence, Temperance, Justice and Fortitude. I imagine as they learnt more about these aspects of virtue the student would create mental images to help store the details and examples given in instruction.

Cicero's description of these four parts of virtue was incredibly influential in Christian culture. They were called the Cardinal virtues and the moral basis for being a good person, citizen and follower of Christ. Plato wrote about these virtues on his book The Republic, written about the year 375B.C.: this is an ancient moral tradition. During the Middle Ages the Christian philosopher Thomas Aquinas emphasized these ideas, and this seems to have influenced Masons of that time. Freemasons, amongst others, venerate the Cardinal Virtues to this day.

So, at least in a loose sense, we can associate the Art of Memory with Hawksmoor's value-system, Memory was part of Prudence, which was part of Virtue, as viewed by a European tradition that included Plato, Cicero, Thomas Aquinas and modern Freemasons.

This tenuous connection will become more obvious once we have looked at another aspect of 'esoteric' thought, things today we might call mind-maps.

Theatre of the World

In the 16th Century, Giulio Camilo was one of the most famous men in Europe. His fame was founded on a 'theatre' he constructed for Francis 1st, King of France.

This was not a theatre as we understand it today, it was more like a 3-D mind-map of the Universe. It was designed to display the order of creation as understood by Camilo, it was a dramatic reconstruction of the cosmological order.

Camilo was clearly influenced by a lot of the 'esoteric' thought that was current in his time. His theatre references Cabala, a form of Jewish mysticism; Hermiticism, an esoteric philosophy, which claimed an ancient Egyptian origin, astrology as well as Christian ideas. His theatre was an imaginative synthesis of these 'wisdom teachings', or esoteric philosophies.

Like all these systems there is a great deal of arbitrary rule-making, his theatrical system was based on the number 7, there were seven rows and seven columns in his mind-map. Later a man called Robert Fludd built his 'memory theatre' using the number 5, cabalists used the number 10: take your pick.

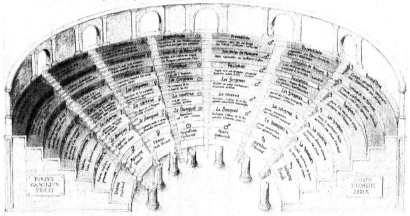

(Picture: Public Domain)

Camillo's "Theatre"

Camilo's theatre was actually a seven-rowed amphitheatre, with each row being divided up into seven separate sections, creating forty-nine distinct spaces.

Into each 'pigeon hole' an artefact was placed that symbolised the power that was being described.

The seven vertical columns represented the powers of Diana, Mercury, Venus, Apollo, Mars, Jupiter and Saturn respectively. What this meant is very obscure and would have, no doubt, been a big part of Camilo's performance in the Theatre, explaining what these powers were was perhaps his whole trick.

These numinous concepts are the stuff of thousands of books on symbolism, and are open to endless reinterpretation because they were vague to start with. How Camilo tried to categorise these powers is not as important for us as to see that he was trying to categorise them.

The rows represented the levels of creation, the lowest being earth, up through the heavens to God.

Again, why this should be seven levels, not four or six, was no doubt where Camilo really earned his money, because there is no 'reason' as such, it is more an imaginative artefact which he clearly had invested a lot of time and effort into.

The best I can do in terms of an explanation of this 'theatre' is to try and take you down one of the columns and describe the sort of ideas that might be placed there.

The central column was named Apollo, who was god of the Sun.

At the top of this column is 'Generatio', so the power of light to generate life, perhaps the power of creation itself?

The next row down is 'Calor', a latin word for 'heat' or 'glow', perhaps representing the internal fire that keeps the universe moving?

Below that is 'Splendor', which might equate to beauty or luminous magnificence? Then 'Lumen' which means *the light*, then 'Lux' , which means *light*, then comes Sol, the sun, and lastly, on the bottom row of this column, comes the pyramid which represents fire.

So light in this system is refracted not into seven colours, but seven degrees of intensity and power, at the top is the power of creation, at the base is the fire we have on earth.

If you find these distinctions vague and confusing I completely empathise, the categories come as much from the imagination of Camilo as they do from observing nature. There are some familiar ideas, but they are placed into a system that becomes exponentially complex, its demarcations becoming increasingly arbitrary.

The forty-nine compartments comprised Camilo's map of the Universe, everything that existed could be slotted into a category and seen in relation to the rest of creation. The images placed in the respective compartments would have been striking, and evocative of their position in the overall scheme.

In other 'memory theatres' different columns were painted different colours. Given this 'theatre' was built for the King of France I think it is reasonable to suggest a good deal of 'special effects' would have been involved.

If Camilo really wanted to impress his seven degrees of light upon people, what better way than to find seven different methods for creating light? Why not use chemistry to create colours and controlled explosions? Why not use mechanics to create movement and scene changes? I think as well as being an ambitious work of philosophy, Camilo's theatre would have been at the apex of technical achievement too. Why else call it a theatre?

'The Round Art'

The techniques Camilo used to impress Francis I with his cosmology were, of course, familiar to anyone familiar with the Science of Memory. Camilo created real loci into which he placed his images. This is a seriously expensive example of the 'round art' mentioned earlier, which uses imagined objects in a fictional setting to order thought.

This use of the 'round art' in conjunction with spiritual, esoteric ideas constitutes a large part of the European 'occult' tradition. Students would attempt to learn from systems that represented the working of the world within their own mind's eye. Developing the right mind-map would imbue the practitioners with enormous power, as they would be working in accordance with the powers of Creation.

These were exactly the kinds of ideas and practices that could get you burnt for being a heretic. Understandably people kept a lot of this to themselves, illustrating in symbols and concealing in allegory what they were really doing. You had to keep your 'esoteric' spiritual exercises 'occult', or you'd burn.

One of the most famous mind-maps is called the Tree of Life, it forms structure of the Jewish mysticism known as Cabala. For those unfamiliar with this matrix of ideas, like Camilo's theatre it is arbitrary and confusing as well as being intriguing, beguiling even, with the correspondences and connections that may be derived from it.

The 'Tree' consists of ten 'Sephiroth' and twenty-two paths that lie between them.

The Sephiroth are lined up in three columns, with the left column representing feminine concepts, the right masculine, and the central column balance. The three upper most Sephiroth denote 'heaven', the bottom four, 'earth' and the middle three an intermediary phase of existence where angels and 'powers' live.

You can see 'Beauty' on this map is the main intermediary point between 'earth' and the higher powers.

The twenty-two 'paths' between the ten Sephiroth are each represented by a letter of the Hebrew alphabet, and each letter also had a numerical value as well as denoting a letter.

Vast treatises have been written about the profusion of connections that this system creates. Words in Hebrew have can be seen as paths across the 'Tree', they have numerical values which may reveal links with words and phrases of the same value, or twice that value, or half it, and so on, and on, and on.

One famous example is the association of doves with peace, both these words in Hebrew have the same numerical value.

Forms of divination were derived from this system. A Cabalist could pull random letters out of a bag containing the whole alphabet and consult the Tree of Life for the separate and conjoined significances of the letters drawn. These were given their significance by their place within the larger system.

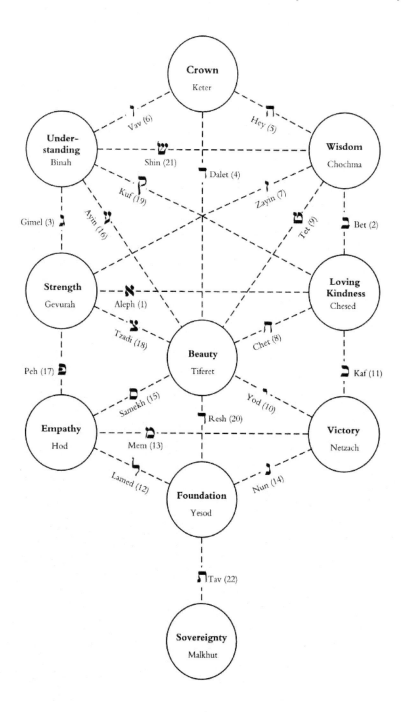

And this system was believed to represent everything, from Creation to Last Judgement, from Earth to the Heavens, from the Individual scale to that of the Cosmos.

The Tree of Life was a kind of metaphysical map, which was valid over all the territories of creation, large or small, physical or mystical; animal, mineral or vegetable.

The Tree of Life was the spiritual equivalent of the scientific "Grand Unified Theory of Everything', and both have proven to be more ambitious than all that useful.

The Science of Memory as described in the secular context of rhetoric takes on extra dimensions when cosmological or mystical influences are added. These 'esoteric' practices are not like body-building, the results aren't obvious from the outside, but they do empower the practitioner.

Every individual has their own perspective: everyone builds his or her mental landscape and populates it with their ideas. Most of us do this by trial and error.

The Science of Memory offers time-tested techniques that I have found useful in my life, for example remembering lyrics I have performed, or lessons I have taught. I have a decent working memory because I have worked on it, it informs how I live my life.

A concrete example would be this chapter, I organised it in my head before I started writing it. Not every word, but the information and the order in which to present them.

Have you ever noticed how few actors seem to become senile in older age?

It seems this might be due to all the work they do remembering their lines?

I hope it's true.

(Public domain)
Fludd's memory theatre
Where you can stage any thing: drama, comedy, romance or farce!!!

Chapter 11
Physical Mind Maps

The Medieval Gothic style of architecture as found in Cathedrals all across Western Europe dates from around about the year 1000. These were incredible works of imagination and skill, whoever designed and built them created something without parallel anywhere else in the world.

Sheela-na-gig, The Church of St May and St David, Herefordshire

Whoever it was who built them and how they gained the knowledge to do it, is not part of this story. What is important to notice is that Cathedrals were full of different sections, were colourfully ornamented and festooned with carvings of imaginary creatures, Gargoyles, which depicted a moral lesson.

They were memory theatres made of stone.

This Gargoyle motif is called Sheela-na-gig, and is found across Europe. She certainly is memorable and I'm pretty clear about the moral lesson.

I think Gothic Cathedrals and churches were made with this memory theatre concept at their core. The mathematical proportions of the parts of the church in relation to the whole, the stained glass, the music, the iconography: these were all designed to *'penetrate the psyche'* and teach indelible lessons.

These buildings were all built by 'Irish' masons, operative craftsmen, some with incredibly sophisticated educations, training that would have taken place practically and orally, not from reading a book.

The Gothic Cathedrals bear witness to the fact these people had achieved something unprecedented; the Cathedrals were celebrations of this knowledge and its highest expression.

Middle of the Sphinx

I played quite a lot of music in Oxford over the years, and before gigs or the next day I'd go check out the old Gothic bits of the University.

It was there I found a book about Gargoyles that piqued my interest. Called 'God's Beasts', by M.S. Tidall, it contains a visual encyclopaedia of gargoyles, an alphabetical list from 'Agnus Dei' to the 'Yale', and a mix of mythical creatures and real animals that are used in allegories of Christ.

It was there I learnt about Sheela-na-Gigg, as well as Blemys which have no heads and their faces in their chests, plus dozens of other weird and wonderful creatures.

The significances of the various creatures contained in this visual encyclopaedia are given by referring to a book called the 'Physiologus' which was begun in the 11th century and added to over the centuries. This book, which influenced masonic art throughout the middle ages, was written in Alexandria, Egypt.

The authors of the Physiologus explain their philosophy by allegorising the most powerful aspects of nature as aspects of Christ, for example, snakes are like Christ because they are wise, Lions are like Christ because they are the King of Beasts, and so on.

The Sphinx of Naxos
Delphi Archaeological Museum, Greece

These loose poetic associations are all used to depict Christ as the apex of Creation, half way to heaven. Each animal offered a lesson in what Thomas a Kempis called the 'Imitation of Christ', by building up a mind map of these creatures each Christian could become holier in thought and action.

The Sphinx, according to the God's Beasts, was made of a human head, lion's body, eagle's wings and hind legs of a bull. This is how the Sphinx was carved in wood or stone in dozens of sites across Europe, the four parts of the animal contain a wealth of allusions and information to the trained mind.

This 'sphinx recipe' links it to something called the Tetramorph, which depicted the same four creatures, but in this context they are meant to represent the four Evangelists, Mathew, Mark, Luke and John.[65]

The Holy Name of God, spelt YHVH in Hebrew, was known as the 'Tetragrammaton'. It seems this system was based in some ways on the importance of the number four.

This image, taken from the Book of Kells, was made in Ireland about the year 800. It is called a Tetramorph, because it contains four shapes and it is a symbolic mind-map of the Universe.

This beautiful symbolic representation of the Christian creed is also a map of the mind, a cosmological world-view, a mantra and a mnemonic. The Tetramorph represented the four elements of creation: fire, air, water and earth.

These symbols represent the attempt to understand the universe on all scales, at all times. They depict the intellectual foundations of faith whilst striving to be its highest expression.

Illumination as cause and effect.

It is also a map of the heavens.

Tetramorph from the Book of Kells

Ezekiel, the prophet, had a vision, in his book of the Bible, chapter 1, verse 10 you find, *"...the form of their faces was that of a man, and each of the four had the face of a lion on the right side, the face of an ox on the left side, and also the face of an eagle".*

Although slightly confused, perhaps in translation, what he saw is recognizably the Tetramorph in heaven.

This makes sense if you consider the zodiac, with the man representing Aquarius, the lion Leo, the eagle Scorpio – which could be represented by an Eagle, not a scorpion, and the ox Taurus.

These four signs make a cross in the heavens, known as the fixed signs, they were the signs that housed the equinoxes and solstices, known as the 'Quarter Days', millennia ago.

Ezekiel had his vision during the Babylonian Captivity, which is dated to around 600 BC. It is pretty obvious where he got his inspiration.

These middle-eastern Sphinxes deeply influenced the understanding of time of monks in the "Celtic" tradition, as the Tetramorph shows. The sphinx was a symbol for the four corners of the Universe, the solstices and equinoxes, it was a map of heaven, the sphinx was part man, part lion, part bull, part eagle.

It is through this imaginative landscape of the early 'Irish' masons we can begin to picture Hawksmoor's Christ.

Telling the Time

In 664, the Synod of Whitby was an organised meeting between Roman and 'Celtic' tradition in Britain, the focus of the debate was the timing of Easter. It was decided the Roman calendar was superior to the "Celtic" one, and so the calculation to determine when Easter should be, the first Sunday after the full moon after the spring equinox, was established.

The Irish/ Celtic church had to stop preaching and go back to their monasteries. The new Roman Archbishop moved his headquarters from the isolated Island of Lindisfarne to the City of York.

The importance of the calendar, astronomy, is clearly demonstrated here, it determined which church would dominate.

Priests called '*Computators*' were charged with ensuring accuracy.

Their role was very, very important, held in the highest esteem, and was, as we shall see, of ancient provenance. This is because Christianity is a solar religion with its major celebrations linked explicitly to the progress of the year.

Jesus is born on 25th December, the day the sun begins to rise again in the sky.

He was conceived, miraculously of course, on March 25th, Lady Day, which in Hawksmoor's time was celebrated as the first day of the year.

June 24th marks midsummer, the eve of Saint John the Baptist's birth, and the day the first Grand Lodge was created in 1717.

September 29th, Michaelmas, is the fourth of these Quarter Days, used in England for religious and financial purposes. Michael, an Archangel, had defeated Satan in the war in heaven and is seen as the protector against the dark of night. He offered comfort as the nights drew in on the run up to Christmas.

These Quarter Days can be visualised as the four arms of the cross, and the sun's progress through them is the story of stories, the great theme that nearly every religious narrative across the world is based on.

If you're unfamiliar with this I suggest looking at 'The Golden Bough' by J.G. Fraser, 'The White Goddess' by Robert Graves, or 'The Hero with a Thousand Faces' by Joseph Campbell.

Here are Mesoamerican, Chinese, "Celtic" and German versions.

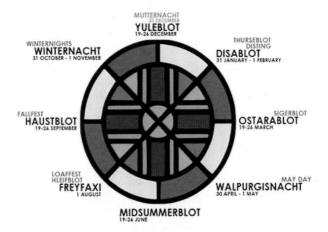

(pictures: public domain)

The Four Quarters are marked in every culture as they are the most important days of the year astronomically.

The winter solstice is the shortest day, and offers the rebirth of the sun.

The spring equinox is the balance or turning point, days will now be longer than night.

The summer solstice is the longest day, and represents the apex of the summer heat.

The autumn equinox begins the return of darkness with nights longer than days. The cross is an astronomical symbol, putting Christ on a cross on earth links man to the heavens.

The Sphinx was therefore a symbol of the unity of the Tetramorph, a creation of the imagination that attempted to synthesise the Cosmos into one system. The Sphinx stood at the apex of a symbolic grammar that was believed by some masons to hold profound significance: it told you about time.

This use of the 'round art' of imagination to encapsulate and distil the workings of the world is of deep interest to all students of the 'esoteric', people trying to build a better map of the territory.

It seems Hawksmoor's predecessors were well versed in its precepts, in their case expressing their understanding in stone.

The broader 'esoteric' movement always seems to offer that elusive goal: enlightenment; whether it was the Philosopher's Stone in Alchemy, or Union with God in Cabala, there was always a big prize waiting for those who tried hard enough.

Alchemical Symbol of 7 pointed star: motto reads –
Visitors to the interior will find the hidden stone

The Map becomes the Territory

Earlier we saw Cicero defined as virtue *"a habit of mind in harmony with reason and the order of nature".* In a limited sense this could be described as a definition of enlightenment. The mind and the order of nature are in harmony, working according to the same rules and limitations. In this sense the mind-map becomes identical with the world it is describing.

In some senses it clearly doesn't matter so much about the details of the practice, be it Cabala, Alchemy, Astrology, Scientology, Hermiticism, Freemasonry, Rosicrucianism, Golden Dawn or Chaos and Magick. Some famous practitioners of these traditions achieved amazing things, whilst some others have gone mad, or achieved nothing of note.

The student becomes the master when he or she has assimilated the teaching, practised it and reached a form of critical mass.

The common thread appears to be the construction of a general mental framework or grammar, into which particular objects and ideas can be

couched. It is the complexity of the grammar that is important, more so than the contents: it is the grammar that gives a broader and more precise framework for thinking.

Whether you learnt astrology or alchemy was less important than how much of that art you assimilated, and how successfully you harmonised that knowledge with the real world.

Everyone has to do this work for themselves, but there are plenty of guidebooks available. Be wary of anyone that says they know the only way to get there; they're demonstrably lying.

I hope it is fairly obvious that these approaches were the fore-runners of what we now call science. They were genuine attempts to categorise the world in order to make predictions and inform decisions.

Astrology was not a reliable method for predicting, but it refined the language and practice of prediction; alchemy was not a reliable method for creating gold, but the practice formed the basis of organised chemistry, and so on.

Though many lives were wasted considering the number of angels that could fit on a pin-head, the language and techniques used to discuss the issue became increasingly sophisticated.

Slowly Astrology became Astronomy; Alchemy became Chemistry.

Isaac Newton has been described not as the first scientist, but as the last sorcerer, he spent much more time working on esoteric matters than he did on scientific ones. [66]

The founding father of British Empiricism, Francis Bacon, wrote about the Science of Memory, saying it was a useful skill being wasted on purely imaginative objects, like Angels and Sephiroth, when it could be used for practical benefit.

Science was the attempt to create a mind-map based purely on the 'square art' of observing the natural world. The 'round art' was cut out of cosmology and material progress began.

Hawksmoor was apprentice to Sir Christopher Wren, a founder member of the Royal Society, a body dedicated to the pursuit of knowledge in the tradition of Francis Bacon: that it be useful, profitable, of benefit to people who would, therefore, pay for it and work to achieve the better tomorrow it promised.

Scientific knowledge was something worth having for its own sake, not a beautiful yet ephemeral artefact of the imagination, but a tangible benefit that achieved work and produced value. Engines, machines, and agricultural techniques: these became the images placed into rows and columns in a new and powerful description of the universe.

This became the talk of the town, how to create efficiency, innovation and prosperity, using the 'round art' of the imagination only and ever in pursuit of profitable expansions to the 'square art' of real life. People were encouraged to stop talking about angels, demons, star signs and potions and start talking about sense experiences, categories, chronology and medicine – so their lives changed.

Slowly the differences between the map and the territory are dissolving, that is what Science is, the approach to knowledge that defines itself as devoid of fictional imagination, it describes what is and that alone.

As mentioned before the Royal Society's motto was *Nullius in Verba - take nobody's word for it.* Test, test, test again; conceptually everything is contingent and malleable, observations are cardinal, the fixed points around which we must build. This figuratively turned Europe's conceptual world on its head, it literally was the beginning of the modern industrialised world. This was the public faith which Wren and Hawksmoor embodied: practical, subservient and rule-based.

By carefully stripping away the veils of superstition science would reveal the truth. Like a sculpture the truth would be discovered by chipping away at error, until only beauty remained.

The Territory Becomes the Map

But there was something more, something that was not part of the public discourse: that esoteric experience promised by all the wisdom traditions when the microcosm, the individual, becomes the macrocosm, the universe.

The Sufi poet Rumi put it this way: *You are not a drop in the ocean. You are the entire ocean in a drop.*[67]

In this sense the merging of the two worlds, the inner, mental realm, and the outer, empirical domain, happens not because the individual has passively 'tuned in' to the universe.

It's the opposite.

In the full-blown mystical experience the individual 'tunes' the universe. As egotistical and ambitious as that might sound this is broadly the description Rumi and others give for this type of esoteric phenomena.

In order to achieve such experiences one would have to aspire to the highest kind of knowledge for the purest kind of purposes; all the

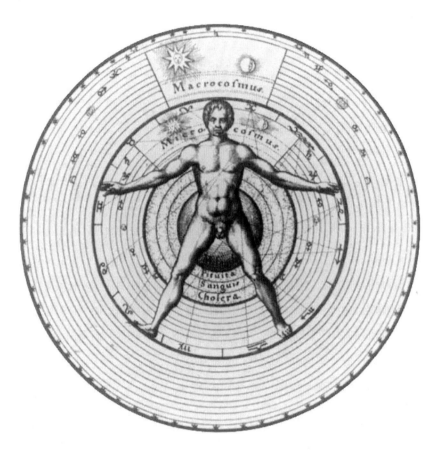

esoteric traditions talk of the 'innocence' of the aspirant, this knowledge cannot be achieved unless the person is ready in a sense they all try, poetically, to describe.

Ultimately the necessary conditions can only be achieved by the individual involved. Although, there is lots of guidance available this needs to be mediated by personal experience.

In terms of the Freemasonry practised by Hawksmoor and Wren I can only make educated guesses based on what went before, and what went before included these types of experiences, where the adept transformed into the master after achieving a kind of mystical union with the universe. This is so old and universal a theme I think it needs no further elaboration.

In the context of Hawksmoor's time and practices we can draw some reasonable inferences.

The poetic and visual grammar of medieval Freemasonry, as depicted by the various types of Gargoyles, indicated that the imitation of Christ was the object of their teaching. Being strong like an ox, far-sighted like an eagle, regal like a lion and wise like a man were all essential elements in the imitation of Christ.

There was a process by which adepts were instructed allegorically, using the gargoyles and parables as memory images to enhance their progress, the goal being to incline the mind of the student toward God, to perfect their mind-map.

There was a fruitful conjunction between geometry lessons that slowly expanded the imagination and the daily routine of cutting stone; this cycle of theory and practice was repeated until the adept was considered ready.

 Then the adept 'died' and was 'reborn'.

From the deepest antiquity such language was associated with mystical experience of the most profound significance.

The Eleusinian mysteries, for example, were experienced and recommended by both Plato, the 'father of philosophy', and Marcus Aurelius, Emperor of Rome. This mystery involved imbibing the 'Kykeon', a psychoactive brew with a disputed recipe. Whatever the ingredients of the Kykeon were, their legacy was clear: the great and the good of Greece and Rome went there in droves.

There are an overwhelming number of examples of sacred brews, found at the heart of Mediterranean religious culture.

The ingestion of the right ingredients would invoke the God within; whether this was done by bread and wine, or by mushrooms and honey: the idea was to harness the power of the Cosmos, to become it, and then to project this Godliness outward.

Amanita Muscaria - sacred mushroom and original Christian Eucharist. Robert Graves became an advocate for eating mushrooms after translating the Dead Sea scrolls... True story!

Chapter 12
Food of the Gods

If this idea is unfamiliar to you then this will surprise you, as Christianity certainly has encompassed a lot of drug-taking in its rituals.

Not the Church of England or Rome, obviously, but as well as in fringe cults, there is evidence that psychoactive substances were used secretly to bring the adept closer to God.

So it is no longer drug-taking, it is entheogenic ritual. The pivotal role entheogens played in early Christianity was made clear by two of the people who first examined the 'Dead Sea Scrolls'.

Robert Graves was a Catholic poet and classicist, his knowledge of Near-Eastern culture was immense, his books display encyclopaedic understanding of myths, gods, tribes, rituals and languages. He was asked to look at the scrolls by Rome as he was an acknowledged expert on religious doctrine and scripture. I guess the powers that be hoped he would be sympathetic to the Church.

John Marco Allegro was a Professor of near-eastern languages at Manchester University and an expert not just of Hebrew, Arabic, Aramaic, Latin and Greek; but also Akkadian, Syrian, Ugaritic and Sumerian. He was one of the world's most respected linguists.

When Graves and Allegro had a look at the Dead Sea Scrolls they both reached a very surprising conclusion: mushrooms. The scrolls clearly indicated to the poet and classicist Graves and to the academic linguist Allegro that mushrooms were not just involved, but at the heart of the religion.

The Essene community that wrote these scrolls were extreme ascetics, living in an isolated religious enclave, they were hardly 'normal' in any sense, they were zealots, and there was a lot of it about at the time. The Jewish rebellion against Rome in A.D.66-73 was a disaster, resulting in Jerusalem being razed to the ground.

There was another rebellion in A.D.132-136, this annoyed the Emperor Hadrian so much he renamed Judea and called it Palestine. Hadrian tried to literally wipe the Jews off the map.

In this context Allegro believes some of the High Priests of the Temple at Jerusalem, now destroyed, were afraid their secret rites and rituals, passed down orally over the generations, might be lost forever. Allegro argued that their solution was to create a series of teaching stories that would encode their secrets, these stories are known to us today in the New Testament.

Allegro showed how there are incidents in the New Testament that make very little sense without interpretation, or perhaps it is better to say they make more sense with some interpretation. This interpretation is based on linguistic devices and puns, techniques the Essenes, amongst others, excelled at.

In Mathew's gospel, just before a walking on water incident there is a passage about the head of John the Baptist. The story then jumps to Jesus asking Simon, who he renames Peter, to perform a miracle with him.

Matthew is very episodic and crudely plotted if viewed only on this level.

In Allegro's mind the authors of Mathew Chapter 14 were clearly trying to convey a message beneath the surface. There are dozens of words and phrases that sound like '**TAB - BA – LI**", which was the Sumerian root word for mushroom.

Sumerian was the mother of many Near-Eastern languages, and like Latin in Europe, was used in religious ritual.

Below I've highlighted the words or phrases that are based on mushroom puns. For example:

'*Baptist*' translates as TABBALA,

'*Charger*' translates as TABLA,

'*A supper to his lords*' translates as MAS-TAB-BA-R,

'*unto the half of my kingdom*' translates as LI-MAS-BALAG-TAB-BA-RI

'*Herodias*' translates to 'little heron' a nick-name for mushroom, as is the name '*Herod*' itself.

Reading this passage would have been almost like a tongue twister, with so many "**TAB-BA-LI's**" packed in so densely.

*But when **Herod** heard thereof, he said, It is John, **whom I beheaded: he is risen from the dead**.*

*For **Herod** himself had sent forth and laid hold upon John, and bound him in prison for **Herodias**' sake, his brother Philip's wife: for he had married her. For John had said unto **Herod**, It is not lawful for thee to have thy brother's wife.*

*Therefore, **Herodias** had a quarrel against him, and would have killed him; but she could not: For **Herod** feared John, knowing that he was a just man and holy, and observed him; and when he heard him, he did many things, and heard him gladly.*

*And when a convenient day was come, that **Herod** on his birthday made **a supper to his lords**, high captains, and chief estates of Galilee; And when the daughter of the said **Herodias** came in, and danced, and pleased **Herod** and them that sat with him, the king said unto the damsel, Ask of me whatsoever thou wilt, and I will give it thee. And he sware unto her, Whatsoever thou shalt ask of me, I will give it thee, **unto the half of my kingdom**.*

*And she went forth, and said unto her mother, What shall I ask? And she said, **The head of John the Baptist**. And she came in straightway with haste unto the king, and asked, saying, I will that thou give me by and by in a **charger the head of John the Baptist**.*

*And the king was exceeding sorry; yet for his oath's sake, and for their sakes which sat with him, he would not reject her. And immediately the king sent an executioner, and commanded his head to be brought: and he went and beheaded him in the prison, And brought **his head in a charger,** and gave it to the damsel: and the damsel gave it to her mother.*[68]

When I checked this passage out in the Bible I found the next episode equally revealing.

In Mathew Chapter 14, Simon asks Christ to call him out of the boat he's in, to give him a name, so he can stand with Jesus on the water.

So Jesus renames Simon as 'Peter'. Peter became known as 'the rock', from the Latin "petra", meaning stone, upon which Jesus said he would build his church, a nice play on words.

But in Aramaic stone or rock is "keepha".

"Pitra" is mushroom, and mushrooms float.

The same PTR root in Hebrew denotes mushroom.

So, will Peter be a Latin stone and sink, or will he be the Hebrew or Aramaic Peter, walk on water, and float like a mushroom?

Jesus, Allegro said, was an allegory for a mushroom. It didn't matter that his argument was a statistically water-tight interpretation of the texts, it didn't matter that he was backed up by thousands of individual pieces of evidence: it was offensive to Christian beliefs and he paid the price.

Not long after publishing his book "The Sacred Mushroom and the Cross" he lost his job at Manchester University, it probably didn't help that he said that Christianity was a fraud and his mission was to destroy it.

No one has ever been able to debunk Allegro's analysis, because it is correct, so it is quietly ignored. Every other near-eastern religion had its entheogens, and so does Christianity. His approach to what he found cost him a great deal personally, but his work, recently republished, has never been debunked – what he found was surprising and remarkable and is never ever talked about by the Church, it drives a stake through the heart of the lies and fantasy that surround the name Jesus.

Robert Graves, the other scholar who examined the Dead Sea Scrolls, took a very different, more practical approach to what he'd learnt. He

Great Canterbury Psalter Folio 1, England, ca. 1200
Bibliothèque Nationale de France, Paris

(Public Domain)

God Loves his creation!
As depicted in the Middle Ages

225

started taking mushrooms, especially the red and white Amanita Muscaria he and Allegro had seen referred to by the Essenes.

Graves publically advocated ingesting hallucinogenic mushrooms as a result of studying the Dead Sea Scrolls. The entire revival of mushroom lore in North America and Europe seemed to happen around him.

He was friends with Gordon Wasson, the former Vice-President at J.P. Morgan, who famously wrote about shamans and their favourite form of inter-dimensional communication, and whose work initiated the psychedelic renaissance in the States.

Grave wrote, *"In 1957 at my suggestion Mr. Wasson and the famous mycologist Dr. Roger Heim, Director of the Musee de l'Homme at Paris, visited the New Guinea Highlands from whence had come reports of a mushroom cult".* [69]

This circle of friends were also among the first to try LSD.

Wasson's work, at one time subsidised by the CIA, was the beginning of the entheogenic understanding of religion, the realisation of how important hallucinogens were to certain traditions.

In fact drugs are evident in all the Bronze Age foundational faiths, Soma, in India, Haoma, in the Zoroastrian world, Kykeon, in the Greek world, as well as Ambrosia and Nectar, all denote a mushroom based Eucharist.

Nero called mushrooms *Food of the Gods*, mushrooms are not animal, mineral or vegetable, appear and disappear in mysterious ways, including the wonderful fairy-circle, and have long been associated with magic, gnomes, dwarves, elves, sprites, angels and demons.

Wasson and Graves' circle of friends made mushrooms fashionable among the rich and curious, the 60's drug culture started in the 50's around these people.

Peak Performance

So at the summit of the esoteric experience the student becomes an active power within the universe, capable of affecting the future, changing the world. All the Great Teachers, as well as all the charlatans, talk about this.

I hope in the context as I've laid it out it becomes clear that if Hawksmoor's esoteric practices didn't include some entheogens that would have been unusual. The example of the Fly Agaric Mushroom being at the heart of ancient Christian ritual, is, I hope, remarkable enough to drive the point home: drugs were used, once the adept was deemed ready, to push the boundaries of experience to the extreme.

Other esoteric practices followed the same basic program, the initiate becomes the adept through study, including, perhaps, some variation of the Science of Memory. The adept becomes the master via some kind of death and rebirth ritual, and this usually included some entheogens.

Freemasonry fits this pattern with its three degrees.

My educated guess is that the preponderance of acacia in King Solomon's Temple is a very big clue to what, if anything, Hawksmoor might have taken.

The Ark of the Covenant was made of acacia wood, this was placed in the 'Holiest of Holies', the sacred space at the back of the temple where only the high priests could go. Acacia was often planted in graves, as a symbol of immortality. It also had associations with innocence and initiation.

The significance of acacia was more than symbolic: it was chemical.

Acacia was known in Ancient Egypt as the Tree of Life, perhaps that's because the Ancient Egyptians liked the acacia tree's pretty flowers. It seems more likely that it was because acacia contains DMT (Dimethyltryptamine) This powerful psychoactive substance is found naturally in the brain, it is also obtainable from acacia bark by soaking it in alcohol.

Isis as Goddess of the Acacia

Ancient Egyptians called their land Khemet, meaning black, after the dark fertile ground around the Nile, the basis of their culture. From Khem we derive the words alchemy, literally from Egypt, and chemistry, the Egyptian people could be called chemicals...

The alchemy of old, the *black* art, of turning lead into gold, is better understood in this light. Al-chemy was the Egyptian tradition of using chemicals to achieve an altered state of consciousness.

Who knows what weird and wonderful concoctions were created?

The chemistry of DMT is simple but its effects are profound explain that the Ancient Egyptians knew of its power is certain. Their Great God, Osiris, the Green Man and King of Heaven, was to be found in the acacia.

His wife, Isis, was a Goddess of the Acacia with her sister Nephthys. The child of Isis and Osiris, Horus, possessed the All Seeing Eye, the Fruit of the Tree, which seems to imply the visionary experience offered by acacia was a key to their sacred wisdom.

To suggest the people who wrote the Bible were unaware of acacia's status in Egypt is ridiculous. To say its inclusion in the fabric of the Ark is just co-incidence is absurd: Acacia had a sacramental role based on its chemistry.

So, it seems likely that if there was an entheogen used by Hawksmoor, it would have been acacia. It fits very neatly into the symbolism and rituals that Freemasons are known to use.

In every esoteric tradition this type of experience is for a selcct few only, enabling them to extend their understanding as far as humanly possible, bridging the gap between earth and heaven, they became as gods.

This is the Christ-Consciousness of the Gnostics; the Samadhi of the Hindus and Buddhists; the Sufi 'Union' with Allah, and so on.

I'm not saying all religious teachers were on drugs, but the evidence is clear that drugs were involved in religious experiences since time immemorial.

The 'Revelations' in the Bible, for example, made much more sense when I read Robert Graves explain the author had been chewing on wormwood – the active ingredient in absinthe – as a way of staving off hunger pangs whilst he was fasting. Absinthe on an empty stomach for a week or so makes the absolutely bat shit crazy story in Revelations make more sense to me: it was a bad trip.

From a series of woodcuts of the Apocalypse for Martin Luther's translation of the New Testament (Augsburg: S. Otmar, 1523). 1523 Woodcut" (public domain)

Then I stood on the sand of the sea. And I saw a beast rising up out of the sea, having seven heads and ten horns, and on his horns ten crowns, and on his heads a blasphemous name.
Chapter 13 Verse 1

"What is that all about?"

Narmer Palette
Full translation – "Moses in the Hieroglyphs", Wilson & Blackett

The Narmer Palette is one of the earliest written messages ever found, dating to about 3400BC.

The palette is said to have been used to mix cosmetics or paints, perhaps this is true, but the palette does show Horus in the form of a Falcon, sitting by some mushrooms, blowing something up someone's nose?

Perhaps this explains the etymological link between cosmetic and cosmos?!?

It seems much more likely that this palette was used in an entheogenic ritual. Such rituals predate written history.

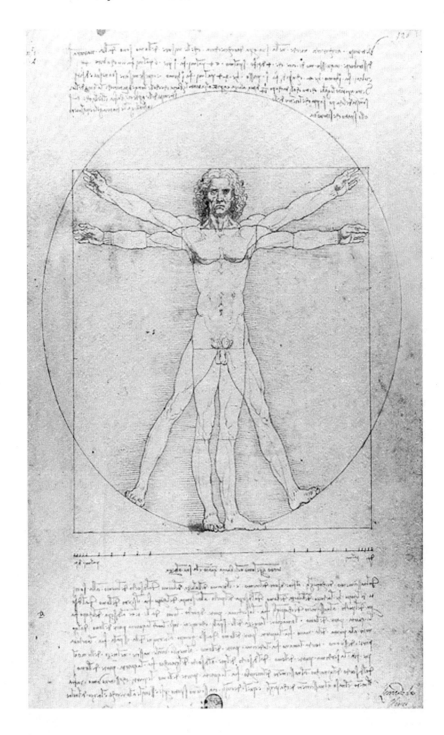

Vitruvian Man

In 1414 a book was discovered in Switzerland that literally changed the world. The 'Ten Books on Architecture' by the Roman Vitruvius was written in the first century AD. It contained a mass of practical information about how various types of constructions should be approached, for example, how to make aqueducts, the surveying process, materials needed, the problems the builder was likely to encounter.

Leonardo Da Vinci, amongst others, noticed the book contained some very interesting mathematical ideas, ideas that were controversial, even sacrilegious.

Da Vinci's most famous picture, called Vitruvian Man, depicts one of the revelations the book contains. Vitruvius stated that the human body was perfect in its harmony and proportions, it was the ideal model from which we should derive the art of building.

In Book III, Chapter 1, Paragraph 3, Vitruvius describes human proportions :

"Just so the parts of Temples should correspond with each other, and with the whole.

The navel is naturally placed in the centre of the human body, and, if in a man lying with his face upward, and his hands and feet extended, from his navel as the centre, a circle be described, it will touch his fingers and toes.

It is not alone by a circle, that the human body is thus circumscribed, as may be seen by placing it within a square.

For measuring from the feet to the crown of the head, and then across the arms fully extended, we find the latter measure equal to the former; so that lines at right angles to each other, enclosing the figure, will form a square".[70]

Vitruvius described the human figure as being the principal source of proportion. It squared the circle.

By extension this set of proportions was found throughout nature, these symmetries at various scales, the beauty they described, were the foundation of good architecture, and of God's creation.

This set of proportions is now known as the Fibonacci sequence.

Vitruvius also describes architecture as the 'highest', the 'supreme', as even the 'divine' art form.

He said that the architect should be well trained in drawing, geometry, optics, history, philosophy, music, theatre, medicine, and law. The Architect stood at the apex of learning, was the master of reality: God was an architect.

Renaissance architects were attracted to this mystification of their profession, they began to use proportion as set out by Vitruvius and some wonderful buildings were created.

In Britain the first architect as such was Inigo Jones, who built buildings according to Vitruvian models. His legacy, of course, has been overshadowed by that of Sir Christopher Wren.

Wren, the friend of Charles II, was a truly an architect in the Vitruvian mould: he was a Professor of Astronomy, whilst at Oxford he had also studied biology, and became the first person to inject something into the bloodstream of a living creature – a dog died. He speculated about circulation and transfusions.

Through a study of mathematics and mechanics, Wren calculated the length of the arc of a cycloid, a discovery in geometry, and he also tried to solve the problem of longitude at sea.

It was only in 1663, aged thirty, he turned to architecture, as the culmination of an incredible early career.

It seems if the Unicorns had had their way Sir Christopher Wren may have been portrayed as a *Great Teacher* with nearly mystical powers. Wren nearly got to redesign London from scratch, the capital of empire would have been conceived in his *sacred* imagination.

Further it was likely Wren, not Hooke or Newton, would have been credited with 'discovering' the inverse square law with respect to gravitation, and would have been celebrated as the first man to understand the heavens, this again conceived in his *divine* mind's eye.

Wren's leadership of the Royal Society, in the rebuilding of London, and less publicly, his key role in early Freemasonry certainly could have qualified him for the role of a National Magus.

But that part was taken by Newton: a loner, cabalist and Whig. For political reasons Newton was elevated to near God-like status, eclipsing Wren; this would have never happened without the Glorious Revolution and the cultural changes it brought.

Wren's legacy was curtailed by political events, after the Glorious Revolution his leverage in government was gone, but not forgotten.

Hawksmoor was Wren's apprentice, and although he never achieved the fame of his master, it is reasonable to assume he followed in his intellectual footsteps. Wren's position as *'Magus of the Unicorns'* was a legacy Hawksmoor was responsible for nurturing into the future.

His churches were the culmination of his career, and he put his lifetime's worth of learning into full effect.

In German they have the word *'gesamtkunstwerk'* meaning something like 'total work of art', it is used to describe an artistic endeavour that tries to include everything, every art form. This is the type of Work Hawksmoor attempted, he tried to project out of his imagination and into the lives of the people of London, to change them and the world into a reflection of his Tory values.

We're now about to complete the circle of this book, going back to what, for me, was the beginning of the journey. Looking at what Nicholas Hawksmoor was up to when he was building his churches.

I hope I've set out the context well enough for what I'm about to suggest he was doing to at least seem plausible. This is definitely the most speculative part of the book, what follows is not a hypothesis, it cannot be disproved. This idea is speculative, but, I hope, interesting enough to be worth your time and effort.

Nicholas Hawksmoor (1661-1736)
Sketched from a 1736 bust by Sir Henry Cheere.
Hawksmoor seems to have been given a look and
hair style very reminiscent of ancient Roman Senators
(KRB – 2020)

Chapter 13
Hawksmoor's Eye

Trying to define Christ, what he was, what he stood for, how he should be represented on earth, was, and is central to a Christian's daily life, teaching how one should live and die.

The Protestant faith made new and different demands on the faithful, it was no longer enough to confess your sins, you had to work to create heaven on earth.

This was the ideology that made profit holy, that made making money a divine pursuit, in contrast to Catholicism's conservatism, the Protestant faith was about forging a new world, some called it the eighth day.

Books, pamphlets and lay-preachers espousing new and radical interpretations of Christian life were everywhere. It should be no surprise that the rich were keen to have their point of view popularised through the printing presses. They proselytised a strong work-ethic and frugal personal habits as the surest means of entering eternity.

The popular press was born.

Access to written knowledge about Christ had been controlled by the Catholic Church, which preached in Latin, so that only an educated elite could even understand it. People had been going to churches for centuries, hearing ceremonies in a foreign, incomprehensible language.

This policy of mystification and enforced ignorance worked up until the adoption of the printing press in Europe. The number of Venetian-backed printing presses is also worth remarking on, they took to the technology very quickly, rightly seeing it as a way to undermine Roman power.

Everything changed once people could read the Bible in their own language: there was no purgatory in the New Testament, for example.

So, why all the praying (and paying) for your relatives to enter heaven on All Hallow's Eve, when Jesus never even mentioned it?

The indulgences, the corruption of the Roman Church, became ever clearer.

The schism in Western European Christianity, between Protestants and Catholics, was central to Hawksmoor's conceptions about his churches.

He had to fashion a new set of architectural symbols, which would define the Anglican Protestant relationship with Christ. The access to English language Bibles, made cheap and accessible by the printing press, had led to a profusion of deep spiritual thought.

Everyone suddenly had access to thoughts of the profoundest kind, notions of cosmological scale and eternal significance. The new printing presses, incidentally, made much of their money by distributing pornography and conspiracy theories. Click-bait circa 1666.

This unregulated diversity had led to a myriad of Protestant sects springing up, and in the confusion King James I had stepped in to place the Royal Seal on Religion. He convened fifty-four top clergymen to rewrite the Bible in English, it is now the most printed book in the world.

The "King James Version" of the Bible tempered some of the extravagancies of the more zealous translations and established the importance of Bishops. It was a compromised remix of older translations and current expediencies.

The role of Bishops within the Church was one factor that later led to the Civil War. Charles I had decreed Scotland should have Bishops, which they'd never had before, to ensure the faith being spread accorded with the King's wishes.

This was top-down religion, the Scots didn't accept it and rebelled. During the Civil War it had become common for the altar to occupy a central position, on the same level as the congregation. After his Restoration, Charles II had insisted the altars be moved back up onto the raised apse at the end of the church.

The symbolism of this is pretty clear, either the clergy were on the same level as the people, as many nonconformists believed, or the clergy were superior, a view held by the Stuarts, Church of England and Catholics.

Form of Faith

For Hawksmoor, Wren and others these complex matters of doctrine and custom had to be given a visual, symbolic, architectural form. They delved deep into the biblical texts, looking for clues as to what these should be.

Many people studied the description of King Solomon's Temple in the Book of Kings. Isaac Newton taught himself Hebrew the better understand the original text and its meaning. They were desperate for firm foundations on which to build their new churches, these foundations had to be consonant with science, and enshrine the split from Rome.

This split had been political and economic in its essence, but was given a gloss of religious respectability by reference to one of the most obviously superstitious aspects of the Catholic rite, transubstantiation. Protestants whipped themselves up into a self-righteous frenzy about that ridiculous ritual.

There is a description of Christianity that goes some thing like this:

It is the belief that a man who could walk on water and multiply fish, who later became an inter-dimensional cosmic zombie can make you live forever if you symbolically eat his flesh and drink his blood, telepathically tell him you accept him as your master, so he can remove an evil force that his father - the all powerful, all knowing and all pervading, but benevolent, creator of the universe - placed in your soul to punish you, because a woman at the beginning of time, made from a man's rib, was convinced by a talking snake to eat the fruit of a magically cursed tree.

The difference between Catholics and Protestants was basically the part underlined.

The fact was that scientific thinking started the inexorable, long, slow drift in European culture toward atheism, or at least nonconformity.

To accept any of the above as fact became increasingly untenable: scientific experiment was doing more in a few decades than church philosophy had in centuries.

Facts on the ground made adherence to this set of beliefs increasingly anachronistic, at best, a tradition no one knew quite how to drop.

Yet there was a baby and bathwater dynamic to this in England.

Hundreds of years of tradition were thrown out as superstitious.

May-pole dances, songs and parades that had been assimilated by Roman Christianity, but far pre-out dated it, were frowned upon in the more austere Protestant religion. Cromwell and the Puritans had even banned Christmas.

In attempting to remove mystification the more zealous reformers also surgically removed the joy and wonder from existence. Hawksmoor's churches are, in their own way, examples of what can happen if cold logic dominates, things get out of proportion very quickly.

Hawksmoor had a deep sense of tradition and this was expressed in his religious architecture. He had developed a 'scientific' understanding of how to represent God on earth. He was used to dealing with symbols, and was deeply schooled in them, he and his contemporaries looked back into early Christianity.

Some of his churches include replica funereal urns, mocked-up Roman ornaments, because early Christian churches often incorporated building materials from pagan temples. Hawksmoor tried to recreate ancient Greek Basilica.

The replica decorative touches harked back to 'authentic', pre-Roman Christianity. It is as though Hawksmoor invented a 17th-century version of mock Tudor, there was similar thinking when the Victorians adopted neo-Gothic, *"Try to link what's happening now to the ancient past, show the continuity of your tradition"*.

Hawksmoor and his contemporaries delved deep into the history of the Church. In 597 St Augustine had come from Rome to convert the Saxons, but there were Christian churches and monasteries in Britain long before that. The pre-Roman Christianity in England, known broadly as 'Celtic', was built around monks privately practising their faith, often in isolation, who, after years of meditation, would share their knowledge with those they thought ready.

Roman Christianity was public, a shared social experience, to which everyone was expected to conform immediately.

No Quarter

Hawksmoor and his contemporaries had very good reasons to have doubts about Jesus Christ as depicted by Rome. Many had read Josephus, a historian paid by the Imperial Family, the Flavians, to create a messianic cult around them.[71] This Imperial Cult was at the heart of Roman Catholicism and was anathema to Freemasonry.

This Imperial Cult was similar to the Scottish Freemasonry as practised by the Stuarts. It was a method for binding important families together around the person of the ruler by elevating their status in a shared mythology.

Vespasian, the first Flavian Emperor, needed to legitimise his rule, the previous Julian family of emperors had claimed to be (great, great grand) children of the legendary Aeneas, who in turn was a son of the goddess Venus. Vespasian was a soldier from a minor patrician family that bred mules, so couldn't plausibly make a claim to be descended from the Roman gods.

Luckily for Vespasian, Josephus, a Jewish aristocrat and general, declared him to be the Messiah as prophesized in the Jewish scripture, this was in 69A.D. This is just after Vespasian had defeated the army Josephus was leading, which had rebelled against the Romans, over gods and money, a few years before.

Vespasian's defeat of the Galilean army of the Jewish rebellion, led by Josephus, made it very clear who would win the overall war. The Romans in the person of Vespasian were indomitable.

So, suddenly, Josephus decided he was absolutely sure Vespasian was the king the Jews had been promised in their scripture. This was near the end of the Jewish Revolt of AD 63-70. Vespasian and his son Titus had been given the task of suppressing this uprising by Nero.

A year later, in AD 70, Vespasian was declared emperor after a brief struggle for power that began with Nero committing suicide and ending the reign of his Julian family.

With his father in Rome, Titus had surrounded and razed Jerusalem to the ground, destroying the second temple built by Herod the Great.

Titus' destruction of Jerusalem was absolute, he left nothing standing, the population was dispersed, and all that remained was ashes and smoke. Across the Empire every copy of the Jewish scriptures was destroyed, deliberately, methodically, the Romans were trying to annihilate the Temple tradition of the Sanhedrin.

There is a famous arch in Rome that celebrates Titus' victory, it shows people carrying off the treasure they found from the Temple they had destroyed. All this is well-attested history, we know what people at the time believed, what they wore, we know what some people had for lunch on particular days over two thousand years ago.

However, the figure of *Jesus* is not mentioned *at all* in any records until after Josephus and Vespasian had returned to Rome and agreed to create their new Imperial Cult, in about 70 A.D. It is possible Josephus started 'collecting' certain stories he thought would carry on the secret mushroom tradition, as outlined by Allegro. It is possible it was Josephus that wrote them.

What is obvious is that as a pacifist leader, telling his followers to render unto Caesar their taxes, and turn the other cheek when attacked – a bit like a western Buddha or Krishna- Jesus Christ, as depicted by Rome, was certainly a very useful messenger for anyone trying to keep an empire together.

Pilate had 'washed his hands' and the Temple Priests were portrayed as the villains. This story vindicated the Romans and victimised the Sanhedrin of the Temple.

Some time after Josephus returned to Rome all kinds of stories started to proliferate about a great teacher who, about forty years previously, had fulfilled the criteria for the messiah, walked on water and did stuff anyone who could write would have written about, but didn't.

This is the point: people from the area and era Jesus was supposed to have lived in never mention him once.

There are references to the 'Chrestos' and similar, but nothing that mentions Jesus by name. This is incredible given all the incredible things he was supposed to have done.

Someone would have mentioned it at the time.

Jesus had made a prediction, about the Son of Man who was to reign after him. This is found in the Gospel of Luke, chapter 21.

"But when you see Jerusalem surrounded by armies, then know that its desolation has come near...

For great distress shall be upon the earth and wrath upon this people; they will fall by the edge of the sword, and be led captive among all nations; and Jerusalem will be trodden down by the Gentiles, until the times of the Gentiles are fulfilled...

And then they will see the Son of Man coming in a cloud with power and great glory.

Now when these things begin to take place, look up and raise your heads, because your redemption is drawing near... Truly, I say to you, this generation will not pass away till all has taken place".

Jesus predicts the destruction of Jerusalem by Titus in 70A.D., predicts the Jews' displacement, predicts the coming of the Son of Man who achieved this ruin, and states he would be the redeemer.

There are two broad explanations for this: Jesus really existed, and using his divine contacts knew exactly what was going to happen and that Titus really was the 'Son of Man', whatever that meant; or, this 'prophecy' was all written down long after the event and was back-dated to identify Titus as the 'Son of Man', thus proclaiming him as some kind of god out of Jesus' own mouth.

The extreme improbability of the former made it clear to Biblical scholars in Hawksmoor's time that the Roman account was not to be trusted. It had been written by Josephus, who had adopted the named *Flavius* Josephus.

The first Roman Catholic Saint, Domitilla, was a Flavian, as was the first Roman Pope, Flavius St Clement. Roman Catholic dogma was popularised by Titus Flavius Clemens, better known as Clement of Alexandria.

These facts obviously pandered to the anti-Roman prejudices of Hawksmoor's peers, but also left them with a problem.

What was real about Christianity if Jesus' story was suspect?

Hawksmoor knew that prior to the 4th century more diverse forms of Christianity had existed, and so he based his churches on the Greek basilica then used as places of worship.

He knew his history, it was in 325 Flavius Constantine had convened the Council of Nicaea, which formalised Roman Christian Dogma. He considered churches built after this time to be inauthentic, Roman temples, not truly Christian.

Protestant intellectuals like Hawksmoor looked beyond Rome, temporally, geographically and spiritually, and found Egypt had been waiting for them.

As already discussed, there were long-standing cultural ties between Egypt and 'Ireland,' and the 'Celtic' church that had existed in Britain long before the arrival of Augustine in 597.

Hawksmoor was proud of the long history of 'Irish' masonry within England. He and Wren had visited Stonehenge and celebrated its creators.

He considered those 'Irish' masons who had brought 'Gothic' architecture to Europe, having seen the style during the Crusades, as among 'those who were curious', which is a curious phrase. His respect for them is clear, they discovered and developed; did not merely repeat what had been done before.

As would he.

He had grown up around some of the most eccentric company in the world, Christopher Wren and the Royal Society circle. Most of these thinkers secretly held unorthodox beliefs and we know Hawksmoor was part of a private tradition. They saw their ties to Egypt as part of their secret heritage.

To Hawksmoor and his friends the Roman religion was a corrupt bureaucracy, a fountainhead of fake news and a centre of enforced ignorance. The Roman religion had been built on a deliberate lie, set forth to pacify and subdue.

New Quarters

Egypt had lasted for millennia and offered, in many people's eyes, the best possible model for a Great Empire that wanted nothing to do with Rome and its superstitious Catholicism.

Egyptian and Biblical metaphors combine very, very neatly in fact. This religious synthesis found its expression in some Masonic rites, as, they believed, they had discovered the true origin of Christianity.

It was all Egyptian.

Specifically it was about one group of stories based around one family of gods.

The Cycle of Isis and Osiris is one of the oldest stories in the world, although it appears in all sorts of permutations and combinations, in thousands of different versions, the fundamentals of the story, the basis for the power of Egyptian religion, were invariable.

The story is deeply encrypted with symbolism and calendar numerology, it works on several different levels and has influenced everyone from Mozart to George Lucas. This ancient folk-tale was told throughout Egyptian history, differing versions reflecting the fashions of the times, but it runs like a golden thread through Egyptian Culture.

This story, what it represented, was the source of Ancient Egypt's prosperity and stability, the myth that founded the longest lasting and most mysterious culture in human history.

The Story of Isis and Osiris was central to Hawksmoor's understanding of history, religion and spirituality, it was one of the central myths of Freemasonry, as is clear, for example, in Mozart's *Magic Flute*.

The story is a cycle, a human microcosm of the moving planets and changing seasons and how, with care and attention, these forces can be harnessed.

Let's us say it is now Spring in our mythical Egypt, all is growing and in balance. Isis and Osiris, King and Queen of Egypt are beloved by their people, the life-giving forces they embody flood Egypt with fertility.

But Osiris' brother, Set, is envious. He hates his brother's love and popularity so plots to kill him. He and seventy-two accomplices trick Osiris into stepping into a coffin, nail it shut and throw him into the Nile.

Now all is summer, blistering heat and wind, Set rules supreme.

Meanwhile Isis looks out forlornly across the Nile, seeking any sign of her husband. She is the home that calls to every sailor's heart.

But Osiris doesn't reappear and she goes looking for him. She finds and gathers thirteen pieces of him together, she finds all of him except his phallus, Osiris' penis.

This is season of harvest. With the help of her sister Nephthys, Isis puts Osiris back together and fashions a phallus out of golden barley.

Nephthys was Goddess for the preparation of the Soul for Judgement. Her magic touch was sought during the final stages of life, her power was to separate the good from the wicked, the wheat from the chaff.

Reunited with Osiris, Isis later becomes pregnant, a virgin birth ensues on December 25th, in the depth of Winter.

Horus is born and Osiris passes triumphantly into the afterlife. Isis brings Horus up in secret, and when he is old enough he takes revenge on Seth, killing his wicked uncle and starting a new cycle.

Horus, becomes like his father Osiris. He takes a wife, lives in peace for a while, is killed by his brother, brought back to life by his sister-in-law and avenged by his son.

Horus is born on 25th December, of a virgin birth, has to escape to the wilderness, returns and triumphs, is then killed and resurrected.

This obviously sounded familiar to Hawksmoor and his contemporaries, this story was found carved into the monuments of Ancient Egypt thousands of years before the events of Jesus' life were meant to have taken place. This proved the Roman religion was a pale copy of something much more ancient.

Eye Of Horus

In his battle with his evil uncle Set, Horus loses an eye. The God of Wisdom, measurement, time, space and languages, Thoth, picked up Horus' eye, but soon realised he only had half of it.

Thoth looked for the remaining piece, but only found half of that, he now had a half and a quarter, but there was still a quarter missing.

He looked and found half of what he was looking for, every time finding a smaller and smaller piece of the eye, every time being left to look for an even smaller piece.

Thoth returns the Eye to Horus. Horus then defeats Set.

Thoth's capacity to tip the balance in the fight between the forces of good and evil are crucial to understanding how Hawksmoor and his friends saw themselves. Freemasons were the modern equivalent of the priesthood of Thoth. They would harness the forces of nature and create a better world.

Glorious Dead

Osiris was glorious in death.

His triumphant entry into Heaven was the Great Hope of every Soul.

The triumph of Osiris made room for the raising of Horus to Kingship and the realising of new potential. Osiris is success; his story encodes the recipe. His message was one of growth and prosperity mitigated by harsh reality and hard judgment.

This is the means to build an empire: base it on plenty.

It is fundamentally an abstraction of the cyclical growth of crops like barley, translated into the metaphysics of a religion.

Put a barley corn in the ground, and if properly cared for, a stalk with a whole ear of barley grows.

Cut down the barley, weigh and assess what is wheat and what is chaff and plant again. Only through careful planning and management will your stock grow. Only through an agricultural surplus can societies feed themselves and begin to develop.

By the understanding of this process, and personifying it as gods to be worshipped, the Egyptians laid the foundation of their civilisation.

They had ritualised prosperity, and were willing to make the necessary sacrifices. This is the cycle I think Hawksmoor embodied in his churches, this is their 'Sermon in Stone'.

Horus was the Solar Hero of Ancient Egypt, and its economy and culture had flourished for millennia.

His mythical journey takes us through the seasons of the year. The story of Jesus echoes Horus', both were born of a virgin on 25th December, both had to hide as children, both died and rose again, both defeated evil and returned to their father in Heaven.

There are so many parallels that coincidence is not plausible. Jesus' story is based on Horus', which was told thousands of years before the Christian era.

In Horus, I suggest, we have found Hawksmoor's Christ. In Egypt he found a Christ that predated the Roman Jesus by millennia. Here he could build the foundations of a pre-Roman Church, based on a 'scientific' examination of history. Christ was Horus, Horus was Christ.

The story depicts the cycles of the solar Year and times of day:

In Osiris we see Winter and cool midnight;

In Isis, Spring and dawn's fertility;

Set gives us Summer and the midday heat;

Nephthys is the Autumn harvest at dusk.

Osiris is north, Isis east, Set south and Nephthys west.

This set of symbols would also relate to the journey of stars and planets in the sky, Osiris was in the sky as the constellation we now call Orion.

The astrology of this story need not concern us, but we should note the significant similarity of this system to the later Christian Tetramorph. The one, it seems, is based on the other.

Head Quarter

The story also depicts the agricultural cycle, the bounty of creation that keeps on giving, prosperity is the key theme.

The secret of Egypt's vast wealth is encoded here. Entropy, chaos, decrepitude and decay are not equal to the forces of love, growth, order and harmony in Ancient Egypt.

Everything prospers, in defiance of entropy. The technologies of sowing, growing, reaping and harvesting, are represented by Osiris being cut down, scattered, grown and gathered together again, even greater than he was before. This is the basis of his glory, his triumphal ascent to heaven.

Osiris gives out more than he takes, so Egypt thrives.

This progress and prosperity were a mystery. How did a corn of barley become a plant? How did that plant sustain a human? How could that human use the sustenance the crop yielded and invest their time in planting even more?

The gods, it seems, are generous.

The Egyptians wondered at their own capacity to create more complex and sophisticated artefacts. They were mystified by this fertility and abundance, how did it all get there?

How had such serene order been born out of chaos, what was making this happen? I'm not sure we know now.

This progress and prosperity remains, I'd suggest, a mystery, in that is there is no scientific explanation for them.

How do atoms become molecules, molecules become proteins, proteins become cells, cells organs and organs living creatures?

Is it all just random?

How does complex order arise out of chaos?

Johnathan Swift compared the scientific explanation - that these are essentially chance events and the result of happy accidents - to the idea you could throw a million letters of the alphabet into the air and they'd *somehow* combine to create a great work of philosophy.

This is still the theoretical basis of the Darwinian mechanism, random accidents.

Increasing complexity, however, runs contrary to how we're told the universe works. We are told the Universe is winding down; having started in the Big Bang, it is inevitably decaying.

With time, we are told, entropy and chaos are more powerful than order and growth. The Universe, we are told, will expend its energy and end, in either a 'big crunch' where everything collapses in on itself, or in 'heat death' when everything is the same temperature as everything else.

But these ideas runs counter to everything we know about the history of evolution, which demonstrates a broadly continuous increase in complexity, with the odd blip like an asteroid or other catastrophe. Some scientists say this is a narrow anthropomorphic view, whether or not that is true, it is what the Egyptians believed.

Are we really just a random collection of atoms that together, randomly, create walking, talking, loving and fighting?

Scientists say our increasingly intricate evolution is just a local phenomena, but apart from that idea fitting their equations, it doesn't explain what we see around us in Nature.

This is a genuine mystery from my point of view, we don't seem to have the vocabulary to describe it. This conceptual vacuum is mentioned here because this is what the Ancient Egyptian priests had noticed, that in the right circumstances you could make $1 + 1 = 3$.

Order comes out of chaos; progress somehow generates itself.

Put a seed in the ground, nurture it and you'll get back much more then you put in. This aspect was of special interest to the priests of Egypt, and the bankers of Hawksmoor's London.

Whatever this mysterious force is, it is the basis of growth and prosperity, and the Egyptian held it in awe. This creative force is what they worshipped, as the source of their lives, it seemed to work for them.

Our modern world-view looks on these same phenomena as accidents.

At the fulcrum of this cycle of progress, stood Horus, the living embodiment of this process of development. He represents the perfect balance of the forces of the Universe, in his person we see their most exquisite expression. Horus was the king, who, with the help of Thoth, would honour the legacy of his parents by protecting his children from the forces of Set.

Horus would become Osiris upon death, the son becomes the father, sharing his glory. Osiris was also known as the Green Man and is celebrated as al-Khidr on the 23rd day of the Fourth Month in Islamic culture. On the same day, St George defeats the dragon, even as Horus defeated the monster Set.

This story is everywhere and Horus as Christ is at the heart of it all.

Horus kills Set in the form of a crocodile *(Louvre)*

St. George Kills the Dragon (12th century)
Photo: N. Kondakov (1890)

The All-Seeing Eye

The Eye of Horus, the Eye of Providence, it has many names and like any good symbol it is open to inexhaustible interpretation.

Here's mine:

Thoth puts the Eye back together at the most critical moment in the story, the forces of light and darkness are in conflict, darkness has the upper hand, at the last moment Thoth remakes the eye, and Horus triumphs.

As noted, Freemasonry looked to the priesthood of Thoth as a model and we need to understand his role more clearly.

Thoth was credited with inventing the Calendar, was the original *Computator*.

The story goes Thoth won five extra days of the year from the moon goddess Selene, these five extra days were the birthdays of Horus on the 25th of December by our reckoning, then Isis, Osiris, Nephthys and Set.

This seems to mean that the priesthood of Thoth used a solar year of 360 days, made of 36 Egyptian weeks which were 10 ten days each. 'Thoth' would use the extra 5 or 6 days at the end of the year to recalibrate the calendar with the sun.

These are the days between modern Christmas and New Year and it was Thoth, it seems, who gave us that week off.

The story of the Eye contains a wonderful poetic twist.

During the battle with Horus, Set gouges out Horus' Eye and is winning the fight.

As mentioned Thoth searches for the Eye but finds only a half, he searches on, he finds a quarter, then an eighth, a sixteenth, and so on for eternity.

Realising he has become lost in his quest and that the battle might be over, Thoth returns the imperfect Eye to Horus, sustaining it with magic. Horus triumphs.

This story contains an infinite regress, a mathematical fractal representation of a truth we all know.

At some point you have to stop looking for answers and join the battle.

Thoth's journey to complete the Eye is a wisdom story as well as an introduction to Egyptian maths.

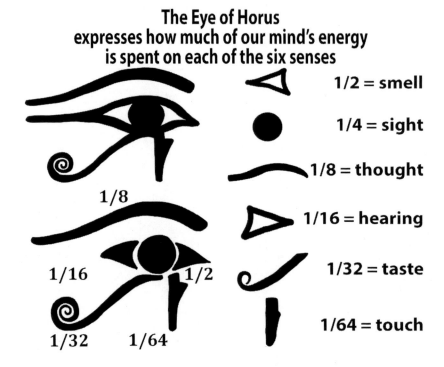

The Eye of Horus
expresses how much of our mind's energy is spent on each of the six senses

1/2 = smell

1/4 = sight

1/8 = thought

1/16 = hearing

1/32 = taste

1/64 = touch

They used a system of doubling and halving and used parts of the eye to represent fractions.

They also equated the Eye with the imagination and attributed different fractions to those senses as they impinged on the mind.

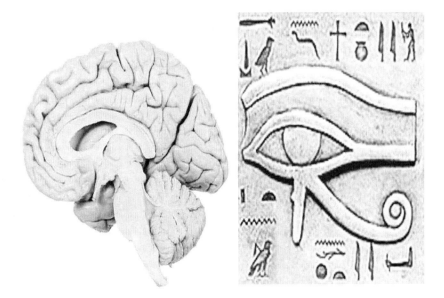

It can't be a coincidence that the cross-section of the brain looks like this. The Eye of Horus represents the imagination, that divine force that can encompass the infinite.

The Eye of Horus symbolises the infinitely malleable imagination being harnessed by focus.

It is the ultimate symbol of bringing order to a chaotic world, it lies at the heart of Freemasonry's mission.

It is an Eye of Horus, I think, that Hawksmoor was trying to depict with the distribution of his London Churches.

Or is it just pareidolia? Am I seeing a pattern that isn't there?

Why would Hawksmoor have bothered to create a tenuous dot-to-dot of the Eye of Horus with his churches?

I'm suggesting Hawksmoor was trying to embody the functions that each Parish had to play within the City.

The character of the area they occupied, their psychogeography.

The different parts of the City have differing roles to play in the ritual.

The different Parishes have symbolic parallels with the functions of the Gods of Ancient Egypt, Isis is in Limehouse as much as Horus in Spitalfields, and Osiris awaits us in Bloomsbury.

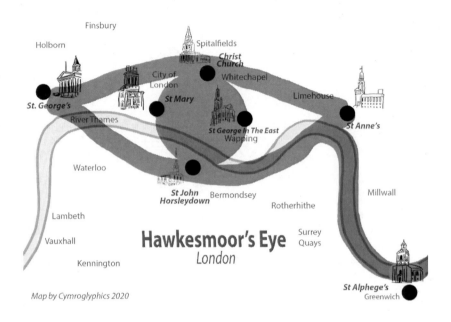

Map by Cymroglyphics 2020

I'm suggesting Hawksmoor used his understanding of Christ as Horus to make the City sacred, weaving a powerful and ancient myth into the fabric of its religious buildings.

As the sun rises in the East and falls in the West, so the gold of the City comes in from the East via the Thames and the riches of trade take root in the West, in the great houses of the fashionable squares.

This money, the profit of Empire, is then sent back East and reinvested in the continued progress and prosperity of business. The profitable circuit continues to turn.

As the summer is followed by the winter, some times are easier than others and the gold of the City was managed with this in mind.

Only those who had an accurate calendar of events could tell when it was best to buy and sell. There was a time for growth and a time for harvesting, only a few at the top knew the fiscal time, where in the cycle the economy was, what was going to happen next.

By managing this cycle of expansion and contraction of the money supply, economic order was created.

The time calculated by the ancient *Computators* enabled their societies to plan effectively, to build and grow.

The astronomical ages, solar years, lunar months, and even individual days were given meaning and purpose when seen through the lens these economic managers. Similarly, the ebb and flow of trade, of profits and losses had to be managed by the new priesthood, the bankers.

This carefully managed process led to territorial expansion, technological innovation and financial rewards beyond those ever achieved anywhere before.

Some in the City believed they were living in the eighth Day of creation, where man had surpassed all the achievements of history and were living in a new and unprecedented age.

This idea found expression in the octagonal spires of many of Wren's City churches, heralding the glory of this God of progress.

'Ship of Souls' – KRB 2020

Chapter 14
The Ship of Souls

The apogee of this progress was the ocean-going warship.

This was the technology that enabled the Empire. They were the embodiment of the state's ability to harness its resources and project its power. They are often compared to spacecraft today, but the Aircraft-Carriers of the US Navy are a better modern equivalent, the height of technology used for the cruelest of purposes.

There was always the possibility of disaster at sea, and complicated legal and insurance structures were developed to mitigate this. Maritime Law, the laws governing international trade, began to weave the web of interconnected mutual interests that constitute global commerce today.

The law of the sea came to be used on land.

As we saw after the Fire, Parliament enacted the Cestui Qui Vie law, which treated individuals as ships lost at sea, who would be counted as dead if they failed to make an appearance after seven years.

This not only allowed the Crown to claim the assets of those who died in London's *Annus Mirabilis*, it provided a legal framework for the status of people before the law.

The language and imagery of the ship at sea extends further into our religious imagination. The body of every church is called the nave, from the Latin *navis*, which means ship.

In some sense the priest is like a captain, the congregation are the crew and services were held to ensure the community pulled together. I'm tempted by the analogy that the congregation are the slaves, rowing beneath the deck, whilst the clergy are beating the drums and whipping their flock into shape...

The vaulted ceilings of churches were based on the ribbing of a ship, the roof was a capsized boat.

The ship occupies a huge cultural space in language and terminology, poetry, imagery and religious analogy as well as the legal and commercial concepts.

It was on specially made ceremonial 'ships' that the ancient Egyptians carried the statues of their gods. It was by ship the soul reached heaven and the sun traversed the sky. Ancient Egyptian craft often had an Eye of Horus painted on their prow.

The ship was a metaphor for the journey of the soul from birth to death, and from earth to heaven.

Like Horus, a ship existed in two worlds.

So, with this in mind, I can take you on a fictional journey, *The Voyage of The Sirios*, and see, perhaps, what Hawksmoor was up to.

As stated, it was the role of the priests of Thoth to put the Eye of Horus back together, to gather everything together and make sense of it, to ensure the triumph of order over chaos.

In London, as elsewhere, this required the balancing of competing forces, God, money, empire and ships, being pushed and pulled through an often-painful process of growth and harvest.

Come with me now, journey into the mind's eye as we follow the Sirios as it returns to the City laden with Pepper from Sumatra...

The Soul's Journey

Every ship had to have a navigator, someone capable of using the sciences being pioneered at the Royal Observatory, someone who could read the lines of latitude and longitude that were anchored in Greenwich.

St Alphege's Church, which Hawksmoor described as his cornerstone, is here.

We see the imprint of Thoth, the measurer, the organiser, the scientist and poet. It is he who guides the ship throughout its journey beyond the boundaries of the known, and brings it safe back again. The limits of his knowledge are the edges of the known world.

Turning north up the Thames the crew of the *Sirios* see the spire of St Anne's, Limehouse, looking out over the water and welcoming the sailors home.

She, like Isis, is a source of comfort and joy, she accepts everyone, sailors who have been at sea many years cry at the sight of her. They are home at last. She stands at the threshold, gathers the *Sirios'* crew to her bosom then encourages them on into the City.

It will be she who waves the ship goodbye when and if the time comes for their next heroic journey.

Moving up to Wapping, the *Sirios* docks and has its guts torn out, the ship is stripped of its precious cargo, which is weighed and assessed for its quality.

In the following few weeks, the Sirios would be totally emptied, cleaned, repaired and then prepared for another voyage, or, if no longer viable, taken apart and the working parts salvaged.

St George's in the East looks over this ritual dismemberment, and like Set who tears his brother Osiris apart, this area is wild and violent.

With the crew now disembarked and the cargo stored, we can imagine an officer of the ship's company takes a receipt – a chit – detailing the ship's manifest up to the markets on the edge of the City.

At Spitalfields market we see Horus, the hero of our story, product of a mysterious union between forces we barely comprehend.

The chit represents the culmination of a million small agreements, the symbols it contains, for weights and measures, numbers and values, are all the product of the cultural conformity embedded in our imaginations. They embody a communal faith.

Without these unspoken mutual agreements the chit is meaningless, it is a product of the invisible bonds of culture and shared values.

The chit could be for anything, amethysts from Amsterdam, or Zebras from Zanzibar. Will this hero be worth its weight in gold, or not worth the paper it is written on?

Judgement awaits, the *Sirios'* journey hangs in the balance. The chit is now in the heart of the City, here, in the stock-market, it will learn its fate.

Nephthys, as guardian of the temple, is charged with putting Osiris back together, for sifting the wheat from the chaff; she sits in judgement. It is her assessment that leads to either triumph or disaster. Will the hero's journey end in an elevation into heavenly profit, or for reasons beyond understanding will the venture sink into oblivion, dragging many souls down with it to a bankrupt hell?

The chit represents the long voyage from Sumatra the pepper has taken, the risks involved, the sicknesses defeated, the storms ridden out, the piracy and the pathos of years at sea.

The investors, ship-wrights, the navigators, cartographers and the Captain, all their work is about to be judged.

Here, the value of the chit is determined and from that single decision cascade a million consequences for the sailors and investors for the ship-wrights and dockers, as well as the slaves in Sumatra.

In the heart of the City Nephthys judges the fate of millions and not all achieve the paradise they seek.

In Bloomsbury, the profits of this heroic cycle of trade are spent in glory. The owners of the *Sirios*, an anagram of Osiris, live here. The houses, clothing, food and wine in the neighbourhood are among the best in the world.

Like Osiris, every man, woman and child in Bloomsbury lives in triumph, every evening the profits of the day are celebrated, every year the lifestyle improves. Osiris reigns in glory, the culmination of the skilful manipulation of natural forces, ensuring an era of unparalleled Imperial Majesty.

The cycle begins again when the profits are re-invested and another ship sails, perhaps called the *Roush*.

Cycle of Life

I am suggesting Hawksmoor drew upon the natures of these six Egyptian Gods to lend meaning and purpose to his six Churches.

I am suggesting Hawksmoor was drawing a parallel between the modern practice of trade with the ancient art of agriculture, as is depicted in Horus' story.

The six Parishes the Churches occupy and embody serve roles within the City analogous to the Gods. Both the Gods and the City are concerned with creating a surplus, for extracting more out of the situation than you put into it, both involve sowing, growing, reaping and winnowing, both are best understood as cycles.

The journey round the churches, seems to echo this most ancient and powerful of stories.

I believe Hawksmoor was trying to bind the fate of London to the powers of nature identified in the Horus Epic.

The story had given the people of Ancient Egypt harmonious progress, glorious growth through the depiction of the agricultural cycle in the characters of the gods.

Hawksmoor, I think, was trying to connect the Parishes in London to the functions they played in the heart of Empire, to harness these same forces to modern trade.

This Ancient Egyptian religious system, which informed their sense of imaginative associations, grew up and out across their culture. Cycles of the day nested inside cycles of the year, within the cycle of life and death, and the passage of the eons.

Though Hawksmoor's churches are stationary they seem designed to harness a natural dynamic, like harmonics on string, and like the *nomes* on the Nile, they remain at rest amidst the chaos of life.

The way the times of day, seasons of the year and agricultural processes are represented by the same Gods is intuitively very satisfying. This mythic system was the basis for millennia of stable growth in Egypt, it also forms the basis for Christianity.

Hawksmoor, I suggest, believed he was harnessing this invisible power, rooted in his secret beliefs, to bridle nature and produce a surplus for the Empire.

Bon Voyage of the Vanities

Looking back on this I have written about Architecture, Banking, Christianity, Darwinism, Empire, and so on through the alphabet.

I hope this doesn't come across as any more arrogant than the people I depict, any more grandiose than what I was trying to describe.

I have no formal qualifications to express an opinion about Hawksmoor, his churches, their locations or what they signify. I have had to look at all this with an *uncultured* eye, as that is what I possess. If my theory seems a bit ridiculous and my explanation verbose, my education lacking to pontificate on such a wide range of topics, I am sorry, but I don't care.

I've tried to avoid arrogance or self-doubt, I looked at that map of Hawksmoor's churches and I saw what I saw.

You now know what it all means for me, as completely as I can express without fear or favour. It's been a great experience for me, so I wanted to share it.

I have revelled in the freedom of expression this language- English - affords, and never knowingly lied. There might be misinformation – mistakes - here, but no disinformation, no deliberate lies.

Ultimately this book is an expression of imagination, that infinite power that sustains and shows us how to grow. There are those that seek to limit the extent of your imaginative reach, they are your enemies, whoever you are.

The most intriguing, possibly powerful, and certainly far-reaching theme that I learnt from reflecting on Hawksmoor's work is the significance of cycles, of spin.

Gravity, the only force at work in space apparently, doesn't explain why planets spin. Nor is it clear why galaxies and atoms do too.

Something's going on beyond the frame of the doors of our perception.

There's a pyramid text that describes Isis and Nephthys as the rising and falling sun,

Ascend and descend; descend with Nephthys, sink into darkness with the Night-bark. Ascend and descend; ascend with Isis, rise with the Day-bark.

This all may seem a bit fanciful, but I believe there is a powerful intuition behind this poetic sentiment.

The cycle, spin, whatever you want to call it – and I'm not sure we have a name for it that properly speaks to its power - is real. In physics this is the *conservation of angular momentum*, a conserved property that doesn't run down because of gravity or inertia.

Things keeps spinning.

This tendency of stuff to spin is, it seems, universal.

The moment Nicola Tesla first imaged the electric motor he said he was thinking of this poem by Goethe,

She jerks and gives way, the day is over, there she hurries and demands new life.
Oh, as no wing will lift me off the ground, you will always aspire!
A beautiful dream, meanwhile, escapes,
Oh, except the spirit's wings,
No physical wing will join so easily!

The setting of the sun, meant it was rising somewhere else, this inspired Tesla to harness the hidden power of nature and electrify the world.

Spin is a powerful thing.

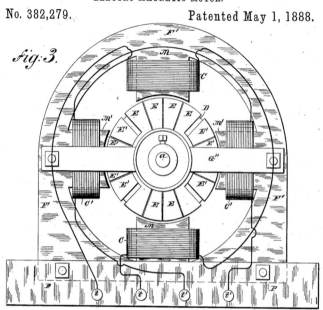

(No Model.)

N. TESLA.

2 Sheets—Sheet 2.

ELECTRO MAGNETIC MOTOR.

No. 382,279.

Patented May 1, 1888.

Understanding the agricultural, seasonal cycle was the basis of material wealth. This developed into ever more sophisticated expressions through the differentiations and variations that became possible once a surplus was being produced. This process generates life and energy; properly harnessed it performs apparent miracles.

London was the latest iteration of this process; Hawksmoor, I think, knew he could not change the forces in play, only harness them.

Hawksmoor cast his eye over London, built his churches to last a thousand years and embody the ambition of Freemasons to bring order to the chaos of existence.

It was Thoth who put the Eye back together, created peace and prosperity from the chaos. As we saw, Hawksmoor lived in turbulent times and he did what he could to restore what he thought was the Natural Order.

I obviously don't know what was in Hawksmoor's head, but it is clear he was up to something, or why would he have bothered placing his churches so precisely?

The meaning this had for him is open to interpretation, and this is mine.

Hawksmoor was a Freemason, Freemason's revere the Eye of Horus as a symbol of the imagination's ability to impose structure on life.

The Eye is a motif from one of the oldest and most influential stories in the world.

Hawksmoor's Churches, I suggest, were designed to give this ancient faith a new home, at the heart of a new Empire.

THE END

Bibliography

Ackroyd, Peter – Hawksmoor; London the Biography; Albion; The History of England Volumes 1-4; Venice: Pure City

Allegro, John – The Scared Mushroom and the Cross

Armstrong, Karen – A History of God

Atwill, Joseph - Caesar's Messiah

Butler, Smedley - War is a Racket

Campbell, Joseph – Hero with a Thousand Faces

Downes, Kerry – Hawksmoor

Edwards, Francis –Guy Fawkes , The Real Gunpowder Plot?

Frazer, Antonia – King Charles II; Cromwell Our Chief of Men

Fraser, J.G. – The Golden Bough

Gilbert, Adrian - The New Jerusalem

Graves, Robert – The White Goddess

Gribbin, John -The Fellowship

Hart, Vaughan – Nicholas Hawksmoor

Hooke, Robert – Micrographia

Hopkins, Owen – From the Shadows

Hutchinson, Harold - Sir Christopher Wren

Jardine, Lisa – The Curious life of Robert Hooke

MacGilchrist, Iain – The Master and His Emissary

Miller, John - James II

Moore, Alan – From Hell

Price, Diana – Shakespeare's Unorthodox Biography

Rideal, Rebecca – 1666 Plague, War and Hellfire

Roosevelt, Elliot – As He Saw It

Shaw, Gary – The Egyptian Myths

Stuart, James – Basilicon Doron

Tharoor, Shashi – Inglorius Empire

Thaxton, Nicholas - Treasure Islands

Tinniswood, Adrian – By Permission of Heaven

Tisdall, M.W. – God's Beats

Yates, Frances – The Art of Memory

References

(1) Page 127, "Shakespeare's Unorthodox Biography", Diana Price, 2012

From top to bottom, these signatures are for: 1612 deposition in Mountjoy lawsuit; the 1613 deed for Blackfriars gatehouse; page one of his will; page two of his will; page three of his will, 1616. In the last signature the words 'By me William' are legibly written, in contrast to the scrawled surname; it is likely those three words were written by a scribe. These are the only traces Diana Price could find of the handwriting of William Shakespeare of Stratford upon Avon. Why are we never taught this historical fact?!

(2) "Dæmonologie, in forme of a dialogue, divided into three Bookes", James Stuart, 1597

The book asserts James's complete belief in witchcraft and magic; it aims to both prove they exist and to sets out what sort of trial and punishment these practices merit, which in James's view, was always death.

(3) George was the son of James I's grand-daughter Sophia.

(4) "Βασιλικον Δωρον [Basilicon Doron]; or His Maiesties instructions to his dearest sonne Henry the Prince", 1603.

The book asserts the "Divine Right" of kings for the first time in either Scotland or England. This in contrast to traditional British notions of rights and responsibilities. James's saw the divine right of kings as an extension of the apostolic succession, it was a religious phenomenon, apparently invented by him.

(5) James I made Robert Carr, Viscount Rochester, then later, Earl of Somerset.
For details of Carr's relationship to Overbury see Page 42, "The History of England, Volume III, Civil War", Peter Ackroyd, 2014. For details of Cecil's role in James accession see Page 1, ibid.

(6) Page 44, ibid.

(7) www.jesuit.org.uk/blog/gunpowder-plot-jesuit-narrative

"Henry Garnet recalled Catesby once holding him in discussion on the theoretical merits and demerits of 'just war' theory. It was only later when Garnet heard through the grapevine that tumults were afoot, that he suspected something was amiss.

When this became clear, Garnet in the hope of foreclosing any action, urgently contacted the Jesuit general in Rome to get the pope to issue a general letter forbidding Catholics from plotting or taking up arms against secular rulers.

For Garnet the extent of the plan was confirmed when one of his fellow Jesuit priests, Fr Oswald Tesimond, came to confession and told him what he knew of the plot. Catesby had told Tesimond about the plot in confession".

(8) Page 166, Guy Fawkes, The Real History of the Gunpowder Plot?, Francis Edwards, 1969

(9) Page 167, ibid.

(10)   Page 44, KS3 History: Renaissance, Revolution and Reformation, Britain 1500-1745, Aaron Wilkes

(11)   Page 193, Nicholas Hawksmoor, Vaughan Hart, 2002

(12)   https://www.freemasonrytoday.com/magazine/9-magazines/160-winter-2018

The differing outlooks and allegiances of these two, formerly rival, orders in Freemasonry is given some context in this article. I found this is from the online archive of Freemasonry Today, which I found very useful, if a bit old fashioned.

(13) Page 52, The Curious Life of Robert Hooke: The Man that Measured London, Lisa Jardine, 2003

(14) Ibid.

(15) Page 53, ibid.

(16) Page 4, ibid

(17) https://www.british-history.ac.uk/cal-state-papers/venice/vol28/pp202-206

(18) Pages 409 - 411, "The History of England, Volume III, Civil War", Peter Ackroyd, 2014.

(19) "Peru: History of coca, "the divine plant" of the Incas; with an introductory account of the Incas, and of the Andean Indians of to-day" W. Golden Mortimer, M.D. Ed. J. H. Vail & Co, 1901. Abraham Cowley's poem "A Legend of Coca" : in chapter I An introduction to the history of coca, pp. 25–27.

(20) Page 477, "The History of England, Volume III, Civil War", Peter Ackroyd, 2014.

(21) "A true and faithful account of the several informations exhibited to the honourable committee appointed by the Parliament to inquire into the late dreadful burning of the city of London together with other informations touching the insolency of popish priests and Jesuites ..." https://quod.lib.umich.edu/e/eebo/A63385.0001.001?view=toc

This document clearly indicates there was more going on at the time of the Fire than we are ever taught. When I first read it, I couldn't believe what it said, it took me a long time to understand the context. This document, for me, is the smoking gun, it shows that, without doubt, there was more to the Fire than pure accident.

(22) Page 177, "By Permission of Heaven, The Story of the Great Fire of London", Adrain Tinneswood, 2004

(23) Page 193, Nicholas Hawksmoor, Vaughan Hart, 2002

(24) Page 58, "By Permission of Heaven, The Story of the Great Fire of London", Adrain Tinneswood, 2004

(25) Page 52, "1666: Plague, War and Hellfire", Rebecca Rideal, 2016

I couldn't believe this when I first read it, how is it that this is not common knowledge? There are entire books about the nutmeg trade

that never mention this crucial fact. If you'd like more contemporary information about this try this link:
https://www.researchgate.net/publication/291522953_Repellent_activity_of_cardamom_ginger_and_nutmeg_against_certain_insect_pests

To quote from this research :"The most effective extract against these insects was nutmeg which showed 100% repellency against all insects after 4 hours of exposure".

(26) Page 410, "The History of England, Volume III, Civil War", Peter Ackroyd, 2014.

(27) Page 223, "1666: Plague, War and Hellfire", Rebecca Rideal, 2016

(28) Page 158, "By Permission of Heaven, The Story of the Great Fire of London", Adrian Tinniswood, 2004

(29) Page 58, ibid

(30) "A true and faithful account of the several informations exhibited to the hounourable committee appointed by the Parliament to inquire into the late dreadful burning of the city of London together with other informations touching the insolency of popish priests and Jesuites ..."
https://quod.lib.umich.edu/e/eebo/A63385.0001.001?view=toc

(31) Page 158, "By Permission of Heaven, The Story of the Great Fire of London", Adrain Tinneswood, 2004

(32) Page 114, ibid

(33) Page 159, "The Curious Life of Robert Hooke: The Man that measured London", Lisa Jardine, 2003

(34) Page 231, Ibid

(35) Page 15, ibid

(36)
http://www.bbc.co.uk/history/british/civil_war_revolution/great_fir

e_01.shtml

(37) Page 411, "The History of England, Volume III, Civil War", Peter Ackroyd, 2014.

(38) http://www.legislation.gov.uk/aep/WillandMar/5-6/20/section/XXVII

(39) http://libertytree.ca/quotes/Benjamin.Franklin.Quote.7EAF

(40) http://libertytree.ca/quotes/Benjamin.Franklin.Quote.8FB0

(41) https://www.livemint.com/Companies/HNZA71LNVNNVXQ1eaIKu6M/British-Raj-siphoned-out-45-trillion-from-India-Utsa-Patna.html

(42) Inglorious Empire: What the British did to India, Shashi Tharoor, 2016

(43) https://teachingamericanhistory.org/library/document/acceptance-speech-at-the-democratic-convention-1932/

(44) https://www.mtholyoke.edu/acad/intrel/fdrwc.htm

(45) https://en.wikipedia.org/wiki/Business_Plot

(46) https://www.americanrhetoric.com/speeches/fdrfirstinaugural.html

(47) https://www.mtholyoke.edu/acad/intrel/fdrwc.htm

(48) https://www.cfr.org/backgrounder/chinas-massive-belt-and-road-initiative

(49) https://www.independent.co.uk/news/uk/home-news/documents-reveal-bank-of-england-sold-stolen-gold-for-nazis-8738805.html

(50) https://www.theguardian.com/world/2004/sep/25/usa.secondworldwar

(51) https://www.theguardian.com/news/2018/sep/07/the-real-goldfinger-the-london-banker-who-broke-the-world

(52) https://www.taxjustice.net/2019/01/23/brexit-and-the-future-of-tax-havens/

(53) https://www.theguardian.com/books/2016/may/29/roberto-saviano-london-is-heart-of-global-financial-corruption

(54) Against Oligarchy, Webster Tarpley, http://tarpley.net/online-books/against-oligarchy/how-the-venetian-system-was-transplanted-into-england/

(55) Page 245, Conningsby, Benjamin Disraeli, 1844

(56) Against Oligarchy, Webster Tarpley, http://tarpley.net/online-books/against-oligarchy/how-the-venetian-system-was-transplanted-into-england/

(57) Ibid

(58) Page 145, The Annual Register of History, Politics and Literature for the Year 1777, Volume 6

(59) https://en.wikipedia.org/wiki/Sack_of_Constantinople

(60) Page 130, The Egyptian Myths: A Guide to the Ancient Gods and Legends, Garry J. Shaw, 2014

(61) The Art of Memory, by Frances Yates, 1966

(62) ibid. Page 25

(63) ibid. Page 33

(64) ibid. Page 35

(65) Page 239, God's Beasts - Identify and understand animals in church carvings, M.W. Tisdall, 1998

(66) See, Isaac Newton, The Last Sorcerer, Michael White, 1997

(67) See, Jalal ud din Rumi, The Masnavi, 1273

(68) Page 123, The Sacred Mushroom and the Cross, John M. Allegro, 2009

(69) Mushrooms and Religion, Robert Graves, available at: https://www.math.uci.edu/~vbaranov/nicetexts/eng/mushrooms.html

(70) Ten Books on Architecture, Vitruvius, Book 3, Chapter 1, Paragraph III available at: https://www.lexundria.com/vitr/3.1.3/cfTen

(71) See "Caesar's Messiah", Joseph Atwill, 2005

INDEX

INDEX

INDEX

About the Author

Robert Shaw has dedicated his career to the study of how the mind works and, in particular, learning more about the causes and remedies for children who have learning and behavioural problems – he has always chosen to work with the most "difficult" children and has had some stunning successes.

His degree was in **Philosophy and Cognitive Science** and after many years teaching children with difficulties is currently studying under the leading expert in this field – **Dr Robin Pauc.**

Robin Pauc is at the cutting edge of looking at how the brain functions and has developed simple, non-invasive exercises and games for children that successfully treat conditions such as **ADHD, dyslexia and dyspraxia**.

Robert continues to work on improving children's lives, bringing more successful outcomes and joy to children that often have very difficult and restricted lives due to these conditions.

During his spare time, Robert has led many groups on tours round his home City of London and in particular the churches of Hawksmoor. Years of observation and thinking about these buildings, combined with his neurological training, has created a unique combination of skills. A combination that led to a fascination with the thinking that was taking place in the 17th century and the message that these buildings reveal.

Outside these fields, Robert enjoys listening to music and performing double-bass having composed hundreds of songs and lyrics, toured Europe and gigged across the world. He has also sailed across the Atlantic as a pilot and navigator.

This is Robert's first book – hopefully the first of many!

Cymroglyphics and the Britain's Hidden History project

British history has always suffered from being inconvenient to ruling powers and as a result has repeatedly paid the price of being suppressed, deleted and new versions written in its place to hide it.

From the Church's point of view the Holy Family fleeing after the Crucifixion to start the faith in Britain rather than Rome has been a constant irritation to its claims to be the originator and centre of all things Christian.

Add to that the British records showing that members of this Holy Family married into the British Royal Line and that Jesus might have survived the Crucifixion and is buried in Wales and the problems are obvious. This part of British history was the first to be hidden although the evidence is still there for those that want to seek it.

As well as the Church seeing British and Welsh history as a threat to their spiritual authority, the other would-be rulers of the islands have also tried to find various ways around and through it to gain temporal power.

When the Normans conquered England with the sword their approach to winning over Wales was to gain legitimacy by marrying into the royal bloodlines, appropriating much of the history and culture along the way and rebranding it as Norman or English.

Henry II tried to demand the "treasures of Britain", King Arthur was woven into Norman chansons and Henry VII rallied Welsh support by claiming that he was the red dragon fulfilling the Welsh prophecies against the "White Dragon" of Richard III of York.

The struggle for absolute rule of the islands continued through the centuries and as different rulers took their turns on the London throne the language and records of Britain were destroyed where possible and marginalised or overwritten where not. The Welsh language became inadmissible in courts and it became a crime to even have writing materials or attempt to print something in Welsh.

Whatever was tried there was still no legitimate way to bring Britain, rather than just England, under the control of the various invaders.

After winning at Bosworth, Henry VII set out to unite the countries under one rule through the introduction of a Tudor dynasty. While bringing together the warring English/Norman factions his only claim to Wales was via the Kingdom of Gwynedd.

The Royal records and history of South Wales was again the stone in the shoe that needed dealing with and his solution was to inflate the importance of Gwynedd and pretend that the British Royal family based in South Wales and its claims to holy descent and rulership of Britain had never existed.

Wales, rather than just Gwynedd, was eventually annexed to England by Henry VIII in what is still considered by many to be an act without any legal basis and has led to simmering resentment ever since. Ever wondered why there is no Welsh presence on the "Union Jack"?

The short-lived Tudor dynasty was followed by the Stuarts and the tumultuous era covered in this marvellous book.

James I saw himself as a divine ruler and wanted to show that his genealogy stretched back through to the earliest times and for a short time at least, ancient British history was seen as potentially useful with people such as Percy Enderbie producing historical works in this period that included such taboo subjects as the British being a civilisation that migrated from the Near-East rather than primitive barbarians that drifted over from mainland Europe.

Scotland had been brought into a "union" and with Wales annexed and Ireland being brutally colonised this was the birth of the English "Commonwealth" that was later to be rebranded as the "British" Empire.

The lengths that both sides were prepared to go to in order to win this struggle of Biblical proportions are truly staggering and it cannot be overstated how important the work of Robert Shaw is in bringing this to wider attention through this book and it is fervently hoped that it reaches as wide a circulation as possible.

The events are certainly not taught in school and are sure to be as big a shock to readers as they were to me when I was presented with the first draft.

The aftermath was that the lion beat the unicorn and from then on could appoint its own tame rulers and rewrite history to a version that suited them. The start of the 18th century marks the end of any official acknowledgement of the British history that had been taught, accepted and widely written about until that time.

The well-recorded history of the British being a great civilisation that had migrated from Troy and before that Assyria was to be reduced to "legend and myth" status and all British historical records dismissed as bogus.

The Welsh, Scots and Irish would all be redefined as primitive "Celts" with their history reduced to a footnote to the massively inflated ideas of a "Roman Britain".

So successful was the promotion of the new history and erasing of the old that the vast majority of the population not only accept the new narrative – they embrace and celebrate it. The English are proud to be "Anglo-Saxons" even though at least 70% of them have no connection at all with them and most Welsh, Scottish and Irish flaunt their Celtic ancestry even though the "Celtii" was a tribe in southern France and nothing to do with Britain.

Ignorance can be bliss and it is tempting to leave things as they are.

The one fly in the ointment stopping this having been a complete success was the famous King Arthur – actually two famous historical British King Arthurs merged into one.

No matter how the name has been lampooned, Disneyfied, transplanted around the world and dismissed as a legend the historical King Arthur(s) could not be made to go away.

Initially searching for only the historical Arthur, Wilson and Blackett were drawn into re-examining the ancient British records for all the other things that had been hidden from popular consumption. They were just in time and managed to reopen the doors of British history just before they were slammed shut forever and people started to forget that there even was a history that was being hidden.

Keeping this door open and rediscovering the authentic history of Britain that was generally accepted and still taught in Welsh schools as recently as the 1920's is what the Britain's Hidden History project is all about.

With this book, Robert Shaw opens another door into the seamier side of British history that had also been closed for far too long.

K. Ross Broadstock

Publisher, Cymroglyphics Ltd
November, 2020

Wilson & Blackett books available from Cymroglyphics

St. Patrick Identified *(2020 – V.v. Orton)*
Discovering the historical roots of the world-famous Saint is the beginning of an intriguing adventure.

The Trojan War of 650BC *(2nd Edition 2020)*
The book runs through authentic British history, shows when the Trojan War did happen, who the famous characters are and it was created by the politics of the Hittites and ancient Egypt.

Moses in the Hieroglyphs *(2019 reprint)*
Having shown how to read hieroglyphs the book goes on to show the burial sites and written evidence for Alexander's short-lived dynasty and Bible characters such as Moses, Joseph and who the Queen of Sheba really was.

Artorius Rex Discovered
King Arthur's place in the British royal family, the fort system created to defend his South Wales Kingdom, the wars that were fought, the links to the birth of Christianity and how this was the world's first Christian Kingdom.

Arthur the War King - *Founder of Britain*
A dramatized account of British history leading up to the birth of King Arthur and then following him as he fights to unite Britain under one rule.

King Arthur, King of Glamorgan & Gwent
An extensive guide to British history from the earliest British Kings to King Arthur and his descendants.

King Arthur and the Charters of the Kings
The story of the ancient British Kings followed by a collection of fascinating events from British history as revealed by the records of the great Cathedral Charters.